THE SECULAR ACTIVIST

THE SECULAR ACTIVIST

A How-to Manual for Protecting
the Wall between Church and State

DAN AREL

Foreword by David Silverman

PITCHSTONE PUBLISHING
Durham, North Carolina

Pitchstone Publishing
Durham, NC 27705
www.pitchstonepublishing.com

To contact the author,
please e-mail dan@danarel.com

Printed in the United States of America

10 9 8 7 6 5 4 3 2 1

Library of Congress Cataloging-in-Publication Data

Names: Arel, Dan.
Title: The secular activist : a how-to manual for protecting the wall between
  church and state / Dan Arel ; foreword by David Silverman.
Description: Durham, North Carolina : Pitchstone Publishing, 2016. | Includes
  bibliographical references.
Identifiers: LCCN 2016025487| ISBN 9781634310949 (paperback) | ISBN
  9781634310963 (epdf) | ISBN 9781634310970 (mobi)
Subjects: LCSH: Church and state—United States. | Freedom of
  religion—United States. | Secularism—United States. | BISAC: RELIGION /
  Atheism. | POLITICAL SCIENCE / Political Process / Political Advocacy.
Classification: LCC BR516 .A84 2016 | DDC 322/.10973—dc23
LC record available at https://lccn.loc.gov/2016025487

For Rob Boston & David Fitzgerald

Without these two gentlemen,
this book may have never come to life.

CONTENTS

FOREWORD

I remember my first time.

The year was 1996 and I was pissed off. Religion was everywhere—my life, politics, work—and I was tired of it, and I mean in a big way. I knew nothing about the atheist movement, and I hadn't connected to it at all, yet. I felt alone in my atheism, but I was sure I was wrong.

So I bought a plain yellow shirt from Kmart and created an iron-on atheist decal from my HP PaintJet printer. It read, in very large letters, "NJ Atheists—The Few, The Proud, The Free." I was very proud of this, my first-ever atheist billboard shirt.

I remember the day I wore the shirt out for the first time. I went to an outdoor mall near my home and sported my art proudly, listening to every snide remark behind my back. There were lots of them. Several people came up to me with comments like, "Hi there, hellbound," and all the nasty looks and gestures (lots of gestures) you would expect. I always responded with civility and a smile, but after a while I longed for a positive response.

Then it happened. On the way back to the car, a little old lady wearing a blue jacket came up to me and whispered, "I'm free, too, I'm just afraid to say it, but I'm with you!" Then she put her finger to her lips as if to say, "Shhh," smiled, and walked away.

I was invigorated. I found someone! I made an atheist feel better! I made antiatheists confront their "demon" and I improved the life, to some degree at least, of someone who was completely closeted and clearly felt alone. I had done good, on my first day. Me and my shirt.

I wish I still had that shirt.

Dan's book is about being an activist, and I don't think there are many more important subjects to discuss. Activism improves society, defeats bigotry, and, in a very real sense, improves the lives of all Americans (or at least those who don't make money off the scam of religion).

But there is more to activism than all of that. Activism feels good.

As you read Dan's book you will learn some of the most important needs of and methods for activism. You will learn how to be an activist and why it helps. And if you read my book, *Fighting God*, you will learn why activism is not only effective, but also morally right, which leads me to one of my favorite aspects of activism—how it feels.

Imagine going to bed knowing you've done good that day. Not that you worked hard, made a friend, or treated yourself well, but actually did good for your country and your fellow human, on a larger scale than your own life. Think about how that feels.

Activism gives me that feeling. I feel it every night when I lie down after having done something hard or accomplishing some goal. It feels great. In my view, all atheist activists fight to defeat bigotry and loneliness, and to make life better for atheists everywhere. And, since we fight only for equality for everyone, we also make life better for members of minority religions as well—we fight for the Jew, the Muslim, the Pagan, etc., because we fight against our common enemy and in favor of everyone's equal rights.

In fact, any way you slice it, atheist activism is being the "good guy" (in the gender-nonspecific manner). We fight against ignorance and inequality, against lies and liars. We wear the white hats.

It feels great. This fight changes your outlook on life. This is not like your job where you do what you do to make money (for you or others); this is about doing good for the sake of doing good.

But more than that, it feels great *that* it feels great. Activism puts you in touch with your generous and compassionate side. It takes you out of your work-for-a-living headspace and actually shows you, perhaps for the first time, that there is serious enjoyment to come from doing good. I came out of college and graduate school ready to climb the corporate ladder, but the happiness at attaining middle management is nothing compared to the happiness that I get when I improve the lives of strangers, even to the smallest degree.

Sure, I heard my share of grief, but almost all of that has disappeared over the years. I wear atheist "billboard" shirts now whenever I fly, in every airport, but nobody gives me any negative reactions now. They are all positive. The TSA agent, the flight attendant, the people in line—atheists are coming out of the woodwork now. I no longer need to wait for my little old lady with the blue jacket. People come to me often to ask about atheism. I can taste the progress.

And I can feel the happiness. So many people call me angry, and sometimes that descriptor is quite correct, but at night I am happy. I'm doing good. I'm seeing progress. I'm part of the solution.

I hope this book motivates you to be a part of the solution, too. You will learn when and where to do what, and how, but please keep in the back of your mind all the wonderful aspects of the why. Not just the *I'm doing good for humanity* why, but also the *this is going to feel great to me* why. Activism helps your outlook. Activism improves your mind-set. Indeed, in a very real way, activism improves your life because you're improving other people's lives, which makes you happy, which makes you understand and appreciate your inner Humanist.

I never saw my blue-jacketed friend again. Maybe her life was changed by our chance meeting. Maybe she told her friends and family and they had a nice discussion about it. Maybe her friends came out to her in the process and their relationship opened up a whole new support mechanism for everyone involved. Or maybe I just made an old lady smile for a minute. It doesn't matter. It all makes me feel great.

So yes, be an activist. You will help society. You will defeat ignorance and bigotry. You will make the world a better place for good people of all persuasions. But don't forget or minimize how much this will all do for you, and how happy you will feel at night, in bed, when you know you're doing good.

Sleep well.

—**David Silverman**
President, American Atheists
Author, *Fighting God:*
       An Atheist Manifesto for a Religious World

INTRODUCTION

———

I meet people all the time who ask me how I got into activism and what they can do to help, or how they can get involved and make a difference. Some inevitably ask how they can make money as an activist. This book serves to answer the first two questions. Regarding money, I will tell you now what I tell them. You can't make money as a secular activist—or, at least, it's amazingly hard to make money as a secular activist, with very few opportunities out there to do so.

I'll go one step further: if you're most interested in secular activism as a way to make money, you are more than likely looking at activism all wrong. Yes, if you're good at what you do, employment or freelance opportunities may arise, and you may be able to make a living as an activist, but I urge those of you who are interested in charting a career path as a secular activist to not focus on money as a primary motivator. The aim of activism isn't to make money. After all, if you're successful as an activist and achieve your stated goals, you will by definition be putting yourself out of a job.

The good news is becoming an activist is easy. You need only the will to make change, the patience to know it won't happen overnight, and lastly, a few tools to make sure you're as successful as you can be. By sharing my story and the story of others who have had great success in secular activism, I hope to give you an idea of the tools you'll need. My hope is that these stories will inspire the activist in you, because the secular movement, like any movement, needs people to take action and create change.

As I will discuss in greater detail, my own gradual entry into secular activism began only a few years ago. The process began when I learned about a forthcoming February 2014 evolution-versus-creationism debate between science communicator Bill Nye and Ken Ham, president and CEO of the Christian creationist apologetics ministry Answers in Genesis (AiG), the mission of which is to "arm Christians" with the ability to defend their faith.[1] Notably, AiG is also the parent organization of the Creation Museum in Petersburg, Kentucky. Thus, Ham spends his days arguing that evolution is a lie and that seven-day biblical creation is true. His museum features a model of a dinosaur that can be ridden by visitors and a display that defends early incest in the Bible. AiG's website says that their primary focus is to provide answers to questions that revolve around the Book of Genesis. On the "About" page, the organization claims to teach "facts." Yet, just as I've done here, AiG puts the word facts in quotation marks, as if to say even they know what they are saying is nonsense.[2]

With all this as background, I argued in a January 2014 piece for the Richard Dawkins Foundation for Reason and Science that Nye should not participate in the scheduled debate with Ham. The article went instantly viral and was discussed on major news networks around the globe, eventually catching the eye of Ham. Ham of course took issue with my article. My main thesis was that scientists should not debate creationists, and that Nye's very presence at the debate would give the appearance that there is a creationist argument worth debating. Creationism has thoroughly been proven false, and evolution is as solid a fact as any in science. Why give Ken Ham, I argued, the attention his organization so desperately craved and, as I will explain, needed?

In my piece, which was later syndicated by *AlterNet*, I wrote:

> *When you accept a debate, you are accepting there is something worth debating. Political ideologies are worth debating, religion, as it pertains to things like human well-being and flourishing, can be worth debating because these kinds of ideas claim to offer solutions to*

problems and they are debating the best way to achieve such problems. Debates about the existence of God can be fun, they are not really that meaningful, but they are a debate about ideas and beliefs and can be worth the effort.

Creationism vs. evolution, however, is not worth debating. Why? Simple, there is nothing to debate. Evolution is a scientific fact, backed by mountains of evidence, peer-reviewed papers you could stack to the moon and an incredible scientific community consensus. Creationism is a debunked mythology that is based solely in faith. It has zero peer-reviewed papers to back up its claims, it has absolutely no scientific consensus and is not even considered science due to the fact it cannot be tested.

Why would a scientist debate this? Nye would do more good on his own going on TV and discussing evolution and the importance of scientific education instead of giving Ken Ham any publicity and a public forum with thousands, if not millions of viewers, to spew his dishonesty. Ham is a snake oil salesmen and Nye just offered him up an infomercial to sell his product. Ham can repeat his mantra over and over; "teach the controversy".[3]

Only later did I discover just how right I was about that last part. You see, Ham had earlier announced a new project he was trying to build, which he called the Ark Encounter. It was going to be a massive theme park devoted to telling the story of Noah's Ark, but with roller coasters or something. The project was having lots of trouble getting off the ground. Ham had overestimated the interest of the Christian community for such a theme park and was struggling to raise the necessary funds to break ground on the park.

Ham knew that debating Bill Nye would be a perfect way to bring attention to his project and really ramp up the fundraising. So he put out an invitation to Nye, who had earlier released a video for the website Big Think, in which Nye said it was irresponsible to teach kids about creationism.[4] Nye accepted the debate and I wrote my article.

While the piece had made a bit of a splash, I had no plans to pursue the topic or engage Ham further. Little did I know, however, that during the debate itself, Ham would attempt to use my article to show how "evolutionists" (a term Ham loves to use as a surrogate for scientists) are afraid to debate creationists because we don't want to expose people to biblical truth. No one really believes that scientists fear the likes of Ken Ham, so his attempt to frame my article in such a way didn't really land, but that one debate moment not only helped launch my writing career—but also my secular activism.

As noted, I had already gotten a lot of media attention for the article I had written for the Dawkins Foundation, but the day after the debate, everybody wanted to know my thoughts. In media coverage about the debate I was mentioned alongside scientists I admired such as Jerry Coyne, and I was offered my own blog on the *Huffington Post*. I was also given regular writing assignments for *AlterNet* (before the Max Blumenthal Islamic apologist days), and even for *Salon*, right before their total blame-everything-on–Sam Harris meltdown.

What seemed at the time like my fifteen minutes of fame would become a catalyst for a future battle with Ham that I never could have anticipated. In that regard, my story mirrors that of many activists who are thrust into a battle that they did not want, or even think was theirs to fight. It is often not what you go looking for that becomes your fight but what finds you. For example, you may hear a religious prayer opening your local city council meeting and decide to ask about giving a secular invocation at a future meeting. Perhaps the council will agree to your request, and your activism will end there. But it's equally if not more likely that such a request will be denied, and you may decide you're going to fight such a clear display of religious privilege. If not you, then who?

In the United States, we are dealing with a religious force driven by people who honestly believe they have special privileges inside the government and around the country to push their version of morality on the rest of us. This force came to prominence in U.S. politics when, in 1979, the Republican Party and Christian Right came together to form the Moral Majority. Founded by evangelical Southern Baptist minister Jerry Falwell, the group played a crucial role in Republican victories throughout the 1980s, especially in the two elections won by President Ronald Reagan.

In many ways the group became a victim of its own success. After two Christian Right–led presidencies, the group disbanded in 1989 following a decline in donations. Religious moralizers put a positive spin on the development. In effect, they argued that the group had served its purpose— it had won. Conservative Christians had been mobilized and their influence on American politics and society was just beginning. Falwell himself famously expressed that sentiment in Las Vegas when he announced the dissolution of the group, saying, "Our goal has been achieved. The Religious Right is solidly in place and . . . religious conservatives in America are now in for the duration."

Falwell was right. Even after the Democratic Party finally broke through and Bill Clinton took office, unseating George H. W. Bush after one term, the power of the Christian Right could still be felt, such as through the passage of bills like the Religious Freedom Restoration Act (RFRA), signed into law in 1993 by Clinton. This bill was said to offer protections to religious organizations that felt their freedoms were being stepped on by the government. While much of the law was overturned by the Supreme Court in 1997, we have seen its lasting negative effects. For example, when Hobby Lobby, the U.S. craft-store chain, sued the government in 2012 over the newly enacted Affordable Care Act that required businesses to offer birth control as part of their health plans, its lawyers argued that such a requirement would be a violation of the owners' religious rights. The Supreme Court eventually ruled in Hobby Lobby's favor in an ignorant 2014 decision, undermining the principle of separation of church and state.

Other states have enacted their own versions of RFRA to fill in the now-missing pieces of the federal law. Such laws are often used by businesses to refuse services to same-sex couples. This is why secular activism becomes so important. Because even though the Moral Majority is dead and gone, it has been replaced by groups like Focus on the Family, Liberty Counsel, and the American Family Association. Politicians, local, state, and federal, routinely cave to every demand of the Christian Right for fear of losing votes or campaign contributions, creating a climate of unchecked religious privilege in the United States.

This is why we all must step in. Although our opponent is formidable, secular activists have begun to chip away at the foundation of the Christian Right's fortress surrounding

American politics. We have won battles from coast to coast in cities and states that are blood-red Republican strongholds. We have shown the American people that those of us who still stand for the rights of every American, regardless of religious belief, deserve equality and human rights. It is an odd fact that those who do the most work defending the rights of religious people often happen to be those who have no religion, including people like me who one day wants to see a world free of religious dogma and hatred.

While I share much of my story in this book, I will also look at the amazing work being done every day in the United States by other secular activists, who fight not just on behalf of those living in the United States but also those abroad as well. Thus, whether you are concerned about atrocities or abuses being committed in other parts of the globe, or church-state battles right in your own backyard, I hope this book will inspire you to take action to advance secularism. United we can accomplish anything, but it won't happen unless we are willing to raise our collective voices and do the needed work.

Notes

1. Answers in Genesis, https://answersingenesis.org/about/ (accessed June 24, 2016).

2. When same-sex marriage is discussed elsewhere on the AiG site, marriage is similarly put in quotes, as if to signify same-sex marriage is not really marriage.

3. Dan Arel, "Why Scientists Should Not Debate Creationists About Evolution," *AlterNet*, January 20, 2014, http://www.alternet.org/belief/why-scientists-should-not-debate-creationists-about-evolution.

4. See "Bill Nye: Creationism Is Not Appropriate For Children," Big Think, video published to YouTube on August 23, 2012, https://www.youtube.com/watch?v=gHbYJfwFgOU.

I

WHY WE FIGHT

———————

What does it mean exactly to be a secular activist?

It simply means you are not going to sit by and let the Religious Right, namely the Christian Right, receive special treatment from the government. It means you're not just going to get mad that this is happening. It means you're not just going to sit and wait for someone else to act. It means *you* are going to do something about it—you are going to *act*.

Being an activist can mean many things to many people, and we will look at that subject more closely in chapter 5, but at its core, being an activist means that you give a damn and you are going to fight. In my case, my fight with Ham had started, yet I didn't even know it.

After the Nye vs. Ham debate was over, Ham wasted no time using the resulting publicity to raise money for his Ark Encounter project. Ham claimed victory, writing a long series of blog posts attacking the arguments Nye had made in the debate and even writing a book about the debate in which he further described his views. Further, Nye had agreed, as part of the debate, to allow Answers in Genesis to sell DVDs of the debate, thus adding to Ham's profit from the debate.

This was the first time Ham and AiG had some real notoriety and, as I had feared most, a taste of fame and sense of purpose. People wanted to know what Ham would do next. To be clear, I was not innocent in any of this, seeing as how I too had begun to write about his every move, but I made this decision knowing few other media outlets would actually question him or hold him accountable for the claims he made.

Through my posts on *AlterNet* and *Salon*, I covered Ham extensively during this postdebate period, focusing on his scientifically illiterate creationist beliefs. I also knew Ham had been trying to capitalize on a big block of funding, at the expense of Kentucky taxpayers. The Ark Encounter had applied for a tax incentive under the state's Tourism Development Act to the tune of $43 million dollars, a request based on the outlandish scale to which he thought he could build the attraction. His application was welcomed by the Commonwealth of Kentucky with open arms.

From the beginning, the state had expressed its excitement about the project, praising Ham in a 2010 press conference for deciding to keep the park in the state, as other states in the area had fought for the park, believing it would generate tourism dollars for them. In return, Kentucky Governor Steve Beshear promised a massive tax break to his group.

The very first real Ark Encounter piece I wrote was for a site called Atheist Republic, where I recapped Ham's attempts to get a tax rebate from the Commonwealth of Kentucky for his Ark project and the project's failed attempt to raise enough money to begin construction. Rachel Maddow's coverage of the Ark project on MSNBC had set Ham off on a bit of a rampage. He was furious the liberal media had "lied" about his planned park, claiming his group would not be receiving tax money but rather a rebate (from tax money).

I saw his anger as a natural extension of his frustration. At that point, the project seemed doomed. Ham couldn't even raise enough money to drive tractors to the field to break ground, and the $43 million incentive offered by the state was set to expire, so I went back to writing about Ham's weekly freak out over the then newly produced *Cosmos* series hosted by Neil deGrasse Tyson. All was right in the world as I started researching other issues that I thought were important for a safe and secular society, which led to articles against anti-vaccine lunatics like Jenny McCarthy. I had no idea the huge turn my life would soon take based on one tweet Ken Ham would send out announcing news I had not seen coming.

Ham and Answers in Genesis had scaled down the Ark Encounter project and reapplied for a tax credit for a smaller version of the park. To my shock, the promise of a tax incentive to Ham was not dead after all. The state had apparently approved an $18 million incentive for the project under the Tourism Development Act, which allows local businesses that bring in tax money to receive a sales tax rebate at the end of the year.

When I saw his announcement via Twitter, I thought immediately of Kentucky's educational system, which had just been in the news for the dire financial situation it was in. I thought about how much $18 million could do for the state's students and its classrooms. And then I thought how instead that money was going to a man who wanted to teach children that every animal alive today descends from animals that had been saved by a man who had built a large wooden boat just before a massive worldwide flood. This is a claim that most children intuitively know is nonsense, but still, if Ham could get to them early enough, I knew he could create more close-minded young-earth creationists.

So I tweeted to Ham that he was stealing tax dollars away from the state and it was costing Kentucky taxpayers $18 million dollars. He flat-out denied this claim and told me that "no government funds will be used to build the ark." I knew this to be a false statement; he had said many times that the millions of dollars the state would return to his group through the tax-rebate program would be used to complete phase two of the park's construction.[1]

My tweet sent Ham on a bit of a tirade. He started writing blog posts about me, saying that secularists and atheists hate Christians and that we want to hurt Kentucky by stopping the Ark Encounter from bringing in millions of dollars to the state. Both charges are laughable and don't merit a response. But he raises an issue worth considering. All other issues aside, is there an economic case for the project? There's at least one comparable destination that might give us a sense of the Ark Encounter's possible benefit to the state—the Creationism Museum. How is it doing? Well, it has seen a drastic decline in attendance since it first opened, despite the addition of zip lines and other non-museum-related attractions intended to drum up business. As a 2012 *City Beat* article details:

> *On its 2011 federal income tax return, Answers in Genesis reported a 5 percent drop in museum revenue to $5.1 million. Worse, AIG slumped to its first-ever financial loss—$540,218. As of deadline for City Beat's print edition, AIG hadn't provided financial results for fiscal 2012, which ended June 30.*[2]

If his biggest attraction, the Creation Museum, could not generate a massive influx of money for the state, why would I think that the Ark Encounter would either? It doesn't seem like the kind of theme park people will travel to from around the world to see again and again like they do for, say, Disneyland. Come to middle-of-nowhere Kentucky to see a large landlocked boat full of fake animals and no roller coasters! Fun for the whole family? I think not.

Our back-and-forth tweets continued. In the meantime, I had also started my own blog called Danthropology on the *Patheos* network, where I spent a good deal of my time criticizing the actions of Ham. I knew that even if I couldn't stop him from ripping off taxpayers, I could at least take up a great deal of his time and cost him a lot of money. I assumed the more time he spent responding to me, the less time he had to manage his museum or to raise money, and that was good for everyone. Basically, as I see it, I was doing a public service. You are welcome.

This type of activity reminded me of my days in animal rights activism,[3] when I would hear about activists routinely faxing sheets of black construction paper to vivisection laboratories in order to exhaust their ink cartridges and occupy their lines, costing them money and time. It sounds silly, but those things add up. Although I do not advocate doing anything illegal, the underlying idea here is the same. By forcing Ham to deal with me, I was taking time away from his workday.

I enjoyed being the gadfly, but I also knew my efforts weren't enough. Like a person sitting in a frustrating city hall meeting wishing some magical activist would swoop in and save the day for whatever the cause, I knew something needed to be done. Taking up a few minutes or even hours a day of Ham's time was not going to take down the Ark Encounter. It was a familiar feeling—I felt totally helpless and didn't know what I could do to change the course of events. Quite often it is common for activists to feel helpless—to think that things are just too big for any one person to make a difference.

From experience I knew such thoughts have a tendency to lead to inaction. It becomes very easy to sit around waiting for someone else to do the work that needs to be done. I therefore thought to myself, why can't *I* stop him from getting that taxpayer money? What would happen if every activist saw a problem and decided to sit around and wait for someone else to pick up the cause? We would all be sitting around doing nothing. The only thing that was going to stop Ken Ham was action, and at that point in time, no one seemed to be doing anything, and I knew I needed to act. So I did.

I realized I had put myself in a position in which I could potentially do a lot of good. I had been researching the project in an attempt to figure out the best angles to attack it, but I had mostly come up empty. This is because Ham seemed, at first, to be smart about his approach. Unlike the museum, a religious nonprofit, he had set up the Ark Encounter as a for-profit business. This entitled him to tax incentives that were being offered to other attractions in the area and limited the ability to attack the legality of the project on separation-of-church-and-state grounds. The park wasn't going to be closed (or never even opened) simply because I thought it was a dumb idea; lots of dumb ideas become businesses.

I asked Ham via Twitter about the park's hiring practices, something I figured he would struggle with, and he assured me they were not then hiring and that they would follow every state and federal law required when they did. They seemed to be playing by the rules; they would have to be, right? They couldn't openly break the law and get taxpayer money, could they? I figured they were simply biting the bullet and playing by the rules, no matter how much they hated it.

This isn't uncommon. Many religious organizations receive taxpayer money, but they must play by the government's rules when it comes to using the money. The problem is, they often break the rules. One of the largest religious organizations that receives taxpayer funding is the Salvation Army. As I wrote for the *Huffington Post* in 2014:

> *In 2004, a group of 19 plaintiffs filed a lawsuit against the Salvation Army. The group claimed that the organization, which is a registered evangelical church and charity organization in the United States, was using*

public taxpayer money to proselytize their evangelical religious beliefs, discriminate, and terminate employees based on religious beliefs.

Anne Lown, a former employee of the organization, felt that this alleged practice was wrong and complained to her management and was subsequently terminated. Lown, who is Jewish, along with the other plaintiffs, contacted the New York branch of the American Civil Liberties Union (NYCLU), alleging that their religious beliefs were often brought into question and that they were threatened with termination or simply fired.

It is alleged that during the interview process, interviewees were asked about their church and religious practices, that those who would not disclose them were dismissed, and that in later interviews they could be threatened with termination if they refused to disclose such information.[4]

A settlement was eventually reached that stopped the organization from using taxpayer funds in this way, but that also allowed the group to admit no wrongdoing, as the employment-discrimination portion of the case was dismissed. The organization receives about $188 million in New York City alone thanks to President George W. Bush's so-called faith-based initiatives program—sadly a program that President Barack Obama had promised to end, but never did.

My piece for the *Huffington Post* continued, describing just how much proselytizing the organization had done before being stopped:

> *For more than a decade, while receiving federal funds, the Salvation Army allegedly has been forcing the hungry to sit through sermons in order to receive the food they desperately need, and forcing their employees to be held to fundamentalist religious standards, standards that have come into question in the past when an Australian media relations director for the Salvation Army implied that gays and lesbians deserve death because that punishment is supposedly in line with scripture. The organization quickly apologized for the official's statement and asserted that it did not fit their Christian beliefs.*
>
> *For decades, it's been charged that the Salvation Army has hidden behind its religious charitable status to get away with such actions, but this new settlement finally says that regardless of their religious status, they can no longer use public funding for proselytizing and discrimination.*

Imagine if this handful of employees had not come forward and the government had continued funding these actions. Just imagine all the cities and organizations where employees have not come forward. Countless religious organizations receive taxpayer money. Looking for a cause to pursue? Ask yourself, how many organizations use this money unchecked to spread their religious message? How many are in your area?

Some states have even begun to fund private religious schools with taxpayer money. They do this through a voucher program that allows parents to choose where their tax dollars for education are directed, allowing religious parents to get their kids into expensive private schools by paying tuition with taxpayer money.

I highlighted this practice in a piece for *AlterNet*:

In January 2014 Sen. Lamar Alexander (R-TN) introduced a bill to the Senate titled Scholarships for Kids (S. 1968 /H.R. 4000). The bill is a nationwide voucher program that would turn 63 percent of public school education funds into private school vouchers. Now, Alexander's bill does not touch federal education money for subsidized school lunches, students with disabilities, and students in schools on federally impacted land or military bases, but the Republicans have that covered too. Sen. Tim Scott (R-SC) introduced his bill, the Opportunity for Individuals and Communities through Education (CHOICE) Act, to expand educational opportunities for children with

disabilities, children living on military bases, and
children living in impoverished areas.

If you think that sounds too good to be true, it is.
Scott's bill is a voucher system for those who need the
funding most. Alexander's and Scott's bills combined
would devastate the public school system. Together these
two bills would turn all federal educational funding
into vouchers and students living in poor, rural areas
and students with disabilities would lose out.[5]

Neither bill has yet been voted on; hopefully, they never
will be. In Louisiana, a similar voucher system was enacted
in 2012 that was supposed to help inner-city children leave
their failing public schools and enter private religious ones.
Why they don't just try to fix the public schools is beyond
me, because the program was a joke. Governor Bobby Jindal
ended up placing about 8,000 kids in these "better" schools,
with disastrous results. Data from Louisiana Educational
Assessment Program (LEAP) testing showed that those
students placed in the private schools scored drastically
lower—40 percent at or slightly above grade level—than the
state average of 69 percent.

Louisiana schools found another use for this voucher
program—discrimination. Blogger Lamar White looked
into the discriminatory practices of the private schools that
benefited from the system:

Private schools, after all, are prohibited from using race as a factor in admissions. But they're not prohibited from using religion or sexual orientation. And Louisiana's voucher program is funding schools that actively and purposely discriminate against children who are not members of their sponsoring church. In fact, in some cases, we're actually being asked to pay more to schools for tuition for students who don't belong to the school's sponsoring church than we pay for a student who does. We're subsidizing a parallel system of schools that discriminates against kids for being gay or being physically or mentally disabled (because private schools are not subject to the same standards with respect to disabled students as public schools are).

These stories are not rare. We must remain diligent and continue to fight against the Christian Right's attempts to use government to push its beliefs. Not all groups use taxpayer money; sometimes groups use the government as their mouthpiece or get churches involved in politics and demand their religious beliefs become the law of the land. This leads the government to grant privileges to religion, whether by erecting religious monuments on public land, or giving special treatment to certain religions during the winter holidays. It also often leads to policy discussions and proposals that are detached from reality.

Turning back to education for a moment, everyone thinks they have the solution to fix our country's schools. Democrats and Republicans fight over funding, and states fight the federal government over control. Complicating matters further, the Christian Right tends to think that the solution for fixing education is more religion. Often secular activism is based around ideas or control, and how religious organizations cost people money and discriminate, but with education, the future of young lives are at stake. The Christian Right does not have a great track record when it comes to educational standards, yet it insists on worming its way into the field of education for no purpose other than to indoctrinate young minds and to perpetuate the position of power and privilege it has cultivated over the last few decades.

Imagine a day when every teenager graduating from high school believes the earth is 6,000 years old and rejects scientific theories like the Big Bang. Our universities would be ghost towns, our science labs turned into Bible study meeting halls. This is not a future I want to see and I am so proud of every single educational activist out there today fighting to ensure the future of our children.

We take on such fights not only to forge a better educational path for future generations but also to ensure they won't have to deal with this kind of nonsense. We want future generations to get a good education and to see their tax dollars used for things that matter. We want them to be free to practice—or not practice—any religion of their choosing without being forced to abide by the rules set by another person's beliefs. For example, I love to think that my kids will never be told who they can and cannot marry because someone's God doesn't think it is right. I want them to look back and laugh at how foolish our generation was for taking so long to end such bigotry. In the same way we look back at segregation and wonder how people could have been so blind and stupid, I want all of our children to do the same when it comes to antigay policies. Education will play an important role in this.

Thankfully, in the case of the Ark Encounter, the challenge to me as an activist seemed much simpler. Ham had chosen to go the for-profit route, and there was no gray area to the law. He had to follow state and federal law or face the consequences. I would keep my eye on him in the event he made any kind of misstep. In the meantime, I would continue to fight the spread of his creationist lies.

In chapter 2, I will explore some of the specific battles secular activists have engaged in over the past few years and discuss how Ham eventually made a big misstep, leading me further down the path of activism.

Notes

1.   Phase two of the park includes construction of a Tower of Babel. I, of course, know the Babel story is a myth, but Ham believes it is true. If you believe it's true, wouldn't rebuilding such a tower be a bad idea?

2.   James McNair, "Creation Museum Attendance Drops for Fourth Straight Year," *CityBeat*, November 7, 2012, http://citybeat.com/cincinnati/article-26546-creation_museum_atte.html.

3.   I reference my involvement in animal rights activism throughout this book. It seems so long ago and it was, as I am sure I have enjoyed a hamburger or two just in writing this one chapter. But even though veganism wasn't for me, I did learn a lot. I am also not usually a quitter, but bacon. Bacon.

4.   Dan Arel, "The Salvation Army's White Flag Surrender to Secularism," *Huffington Post*, March 21, 2014, http://www.huffingtonpost.com/dan-arel/the-salvation-armys-white-flag-surrender-to-secularism_b_5003298.html.

5.   Dan Arel, "Why Religious Fundamentalists Are So Excited about Charter Schools," *AlterNet*, March 24, 2016, http://www.alternet.org/belief/why-religious-fundamentalists-are-some-biggest-beneficiaries-charter-schools.

2

ACTIVISM IN ACTION

One of the best examples of secular activism at work comes from people requesting to give secular invocations at local government meetings in place of religious ones. Across the country, many such meetings typically begin with prayers from religious groups, usually Christian. Such requests are not new, but they are perhaps of even greater significance today given the Supreme Court's ruling in *Town of Greece v. Galloway*. In February 2008, Susan Galloway and Linda Stephens, represented by Americans United for the Separation of Church and State, challenged this practice by suing the town of Greece, New York, arguing that its opening prayers violated the establishment clause of the U.S. Constitution. The case made it to the Supreme Court, and in May 2015, the court ruled in favor of religion, upholding opening sectarian prayers in government meetings as constitutional.

The majority opinion stated, "The town of Greece does not violate the First Amendment by opening its meetings with prayer that comports with our tradition and does not coerce participation by nonadherence." The ruling even went as far as to say that prayers at government meetings are permissible under the constitution. "To hold that invocations must be nonsectarian would force the legislatures sponsoring prayers and the courts deciding these cases to act as supervisors and censors of religious speech," wrote Justice Anthony Kennedy.

The dissenting opinion, however, called attention to the fact that the town of Greece showed preferential treatment to one single religion, a clear violation of the establishment clause as argued by the plaintiffs. "So month in and month out for over a decade, prayers steeped in only one faith, addressed toward members of the public, commenced meetings to discuss local affairs and distribute government benefits. In my view, that practice does not square with the First Amendment's promise that every citizen, irrespective of her religion, owns an equal share in her government," wrote Justice Elena Kagan.[1]

The ruling was widely opposed not only by secular, humanist, and atheist groups but also by the American Jewish Committee and the Anti-Defamation League. Daniel Mach, director of the American Civil Liberties Union (ACLU) Program on Freedom of Religion and Belief, said in a statement that the organization was "disappointed" by the decision, adding, "Official religious favoritism should be off-limits under the Constitution. Town-sponsored sectarian prayer violates the basic rule requiring the government to stay neutral on matters of faith."

A year earlier Arizona State Representative Juan Mendez made national headlines by not only coming out as an atheist in public office but also by delivering a secular invocation at the daily Arizona House of Representatives invocation. During it, he asked legislators to look at each other rather than bow their heads so they might "celebrate our shared humanness." The act was so upsetting to Republican Representative Steve Smith that the following day he delivered two prayers in an attempt to make up for the one he said they had missed the day before, adding that Mendez should have skipped his turn if he was not going to stick to tradition and offer a traditional prayer.

Smith's actions did not come without backlash from the secular community, as he got the attention of American Atheists, one of the largest atheist nonprofit groups in the United States. "Opening the legislative sessions with prayer is disenfranchising to anyone who is not Christian as demonstrated by Representative Mendez' attempt to balance this outdated practice with a secular alternative," said David Silverman, president of American Atheists. "But for Representative Smith to say that a fellow lawmaker's secular choice requires 'repentance' is reprehensible. His statement excluding nonbelievers is one of the most un-American remarks I have ever heard from a public servant and is a perfect example of why there should not be any prayer sponsored by the government. Senator Smith should be ashamed. He owes Representative Mendez an apology. He owes non-Christians an apology. He owes the American people an apology."[2]

One high-profile Arizona resident similarly denounced Smith's words. "State Representative Steve Smith embarrassed himself. . . . [he] demonstrated how, unfortunately, religious belief can be used as a basis for exclusion and hatred. Our Constitution guarantees equal protection and rights to all people, regardless of their religious beliefs or lack of religious beliefs. Senator Smith owes Representative Mendez, and the citizens of our state, an apology for his inappropriate remarks," said Lawrence Krauss, Foundation Professor of the School of Earth and Space Exploration at Arizona State University.

In an interview with Religion News Service, Mendez explained why his simple action was needed: "Too many people feel disenfranchised from civic engagement and social justice work because they don't see their values articulated by their government representatives, their community leaders, their neighbors or their friends. But Humanist and other secular invocations can be relevant and resonant for everyone, regardless of religious belief or nonbelief."[3]

He stressed, however, that secular invocations are important not only for recognizing atheists, but also for buttressing the religious freedom of all theists: "People of faith need to support the full variety of expressions of belief and nonbelief in our communities because it's essential to religious freedom. This freedom applies to all of us—not just those whose religion is in the majority at any given moment. The healthiest thing for our democracy would be to begin our public meetings with statements that focus all of us, regardless of religious belief or nonreligious worldview, on the collaborative work of representing our constituents and improving our world."

Mendez's actions helped inspire secular activists across the country, including in Florida, North Carolina, and Illinois. These activists saw one religion getting all the attention during opening prayers. Instead of waiting for another Mendez to act, they decided they would be the ones to step in.

One of my first entries into secular activism involved the highly controversial cross that was soon set to be displayed at the 9/11 Museum in New York. I described the issue at hand in a May 2014 *Huffington Post* article I wrote on the topic:

> *When you build a skyscraper using steel beams you build it using crossbeams. When these buildings come down, there is a high chance some of those crossbeams will remain standing.*

When two planes took down the World Trade Center towers on September 11, 2001, it should really be of no surprise steel crosses were left standing.

What should be a surprise is that someone pulled one of these from the rubble, had it then cut to look more like the Latin cross worshiped by Christians around the world, blessed by a priest and then called a "miracle."

This cross is a manmade symbol of Christian worship. It does not symbolize anything of significance in the history of the attacks on 9/11 and it has no place in a 9/11 museum on its own. When the 9/11 Museum in New York City announced its plans to include this cross in the museum's memorial, it should be as no surprise that American Atheists took offense and filed a lawsuit to stand up for Americans' First Amendment rights.[4]

National news networks and even Comedy Central's *Colbert Report* covered American Atheists' lawsuit against the cross's inclusion. Many Americans, even many atheists, thought the case was pointless and argued that American Atheists should drop it and just let the cross be in the museum. I, however, did not share this view. I saw a much bigger battle at hand and rejected the idea that the case was filed simply for the sake of those atheists offended by the Christian cross.

The museum had already given into pressure from other

religious groups and agreed to include symbols representing Jewish and Hindu victims, while at the same time blatantly ignoring the memory of nonbelievers. Indeed, based on population statistics, we know that hundreds of nonbelievers were killed on 9/11, and they were not being represented.

As I wrote in the *Huffington Post* piece, this was a case of clear-cut discrimination:

> *American Atheists president David Silverman visited Fox News' Megyn Kelly and she laughed off the claim that atheists were being discriminated against. [She claimed] that this cross was found in the rubble and no atheist symbol was found. . . . Yet she had nothing to say about the planned inclusion of Jewish and Hindu symbols that had not been found on the grounds of the World Trade Center.*
>
> *Kelly berated Silverman demanding he prove atheists suffer from dyspepsia and headaches from being forced to look at this cross. She clearly missed the point of the entire lawsuit and only wanted to focus her attention on demeaning the lives of atheists lost in those attacks. . . . Silverman tried to explain that atheists do not suffer those symptoms from simply seeing the cross, yet do suffer from remembering those terrible events while at the same time facing religious discrimination [and that] it would be of no surprise they would suffer*

from physical and psychological distress.

If American Atheists hadn't acted, yet another precedent would have been set without resistance. At the time I wrote the article I had no affiliation with or connection to the organization beyond a few unrelated email exchanges with Pamela Whissel, the editor-in-chief of *American Atheist*, in which I pitched a new column for the magazine. A few days after I had posted the article I got an email from Pam letting me know she had shown the article to the American Atheists lawyer who was fighting the 9/11 case, Edwin Kagin, and his comment was simply, "He gets it!"

That email was sent to me on March 12, 2014, and I was elated. I knew of Kagin and was a great admirer of his work. To know that he had read something I wrote and liked it meant a lot to me. On March 28, just two weeks later, I got an email informing me of Kagin's passing. His loss was a huge blow to the atheist and secular movement. His legacy will have a lasting impact for generations to come and we all owe him a debt of gratitude for his selfless work.

It was then that I knew I wanted to continue in this movement. I knew my experience in activism and my desire to make the world a better place had found a home. The community was welcoming and the United States was in a strange place. You could feel the Christian Right trying to tighten its grip on the world it was losing control of. This attitude drove me to continue to investigate the Ark Encounter project even after Ham said the project was on the legal up and up. I didn't simply take his word for it.

In numerous interviews and posts, Ham referred to the Ark Encounter as a ministry, which led me to wonder how a for-profit company could work as a ministry if, let's say as an atheist, I decided to apply for a job there. Would I be denied employment from his for-profit ministry for not having the same religious beliefs? To deny for-profit employment based on religious grounds would be a violation of federal law under the Equal Opportunity Employment Act.

I knew if I wanted to do damage, I would need to keep digging. I would need to put in the long hours combing through documents generously provided to me by secular activists in Kentucky who had acquired mountains of paperwork through the Freedom of Information Act. Unfortunately, the paperwork didn't have the smoking gun I needed. Much of the information in the documents was by then already common knowledge or at least assumed, such as details about who owned the Ark Encounter and who would run it. Most people already figured Answers in Genesis would run the whole show, as it had been the face of the project for years.

By now, Americans United for the Separation of Church and State had been discussing the project on its site and seeking the same kind of smoking gun I was. Ham has a history of saying one thing, doing another, and then justifying his actions by quoting the Bible. He then cries that secularists are attacking him, calls secularism a religion, and proceeds to ask for donations. Thus, they also knew Ken Ham's words could not be trusted, but there needed to be proof; we needed to find whatever he was hiding.

Although I realized it would be uncharacteristic of Ham to break the law, I also knew this: many among the Christian Right do not abide by "man-made" laws. They often defer to God's laws, or, in reality, whatever interpretation of the Bible they can swing to justify their actions, and use their religious beliefs as an excuse for breaking whatever actual laws they broke. We saw this following the same-sex marriage ruling, when county clerks, governors, and even judges tried to ignore the Supreme Court, claiming it cannot overrule God's laws. It's funny that God's laws always seem to be exactly the same as what the Christian Right need them to be.

When digging for malfeasance, you often have to dig in the places you least expect to find what you're looking for. The answers are rarely right in front of you. I spent years doing animal rights activism,[5] working with groups to expose illegalities, such as companies testing beauty products on animals, and lobbying to make factory farms safer and more humane. I learned that most of what these companies do is perfectly legal, but they have weaknesses. They need to turn a profit and, knowing there is little oversight on their practices, will sometimes cut corners to do so. When you discover an illegal practice, you can crumble a laboratory to the ground.

When I left animal rights activism, I took a lot of what I learned with me. I use that knowledge today when defending religious freedom and secular rights. I knew I was not going to find Ham's weakness in the corporate documents, or in how the business was set up. They had lawyers for that and they would likely make sure every "t" was crossed and "i" dotted. And then I realized the answer was probably not in the Ark Encounter, but likely sitting inside Answers in Genesis, the organization running the whole show.

While browsing the AiG website looking for mentions of the Ark Encounter, I clicked on the "careers" page—partly out of boredom, and partly out of curiosity as to what kind of positions AiG needed to fill. I imagined a posting for a scientist in which the only requirement was something like, "Must be willing to lie with conviction." Or perhaps a posting for a docent with a requirement that read, "Must be able to explain how incest is okay as long as it's biblically based." But what I found was way more exciting.

I found a job opening for a CAD designer, someone who creates blueprints for construction. The posting's title read: "CAD Technician Designer, Ark Encounter." My first thought was, why is AiG hiring for the Ark Encounter when the park is a separate, for-profit business entity? The position description began: "Our work at Ark Encounter is more than a job, it is also a ministry." This didn't make sense, but as I read further, it just got weirder. It went on to describe how the job would involve doing God's work. It also stated clearly that in order to be hired for the job, you must sign a statement of faith, a salvation testimony, and a creation belief statement. Can you imagine applying for a job at Walmart in which the company demanded that these things be signed? Or required that you sign a statement affirming your commitment to the religion of Ayn Rand–style capitalism?

I had found it. The smoking gun I needed. I knew AiG must be breaking the law if it was requiring all of this of potential employees in a for-profit company. How could Ham defend this when he clearly told me that the park would follow all state and federal hiring practices? The law could not be clearer. According to the U.S. Equal Employment Opportunity Commission,

> *Religious discrimination involves treating a person (an applicant or employee) unfavorably because of his or her religious beliefs. The law protects not only people who belong to traditional, organized religions, such as Buddhism, Christianity, Hinduism, Islam, and Judaism, but also others who have sincerely held religious, ethical, or moral beliefs.*

It then plainly states:

The law forbids discrimination when it comes to any aspect of employment, including hiring, firing, pay, job assignments, promotions, layoff, training, fringe benefits, and any other term or condition of employment.[6]

The law was clearly being broken, and I needed to do something about it. But before I could even act, a unique opportunity arose. Ham tweeted out that he was going to be appearing on a Christian radio program called CrossTalk to discuss the recent articles that had been posted about the Ark Encounter—more specifically, ones I had written. I knew what I had to do; I had to get on the air with him.

I called more than thirty times before someone answered. I told the man on the phone that Ham was discussing me on the radio and that I would like to ask him some questions. He asked me to hold and then suddenly I was on the air. I scrambled to get my thoughts together.

I decided first to ask Ham to explain some of the conflicting comments he had made, like telling everyone that the theme park would not be receiving any money from the state for its development but then saying the state would pay the park a "fee" for the tourism it brought in. Ham responded by claiming he would bring in millions of dollars to the state and cited a *not-for-public-eyes* study that verified his claims.

With the warm-up over, I then decided to turn to the big question: I asked him about the religious discrimination in their hiring practices that I had just recently discovered. He quickly replied, "You don't know what you are talking about," and told me the park was not hiring anyone. I then heard a click and the phone call was over, and I immediately heard the radio announcer proclaim that it sounded like I needed to do my homework.

Joshua Kelly, my talented friend and author of *Oh, Your god!*, called right after me. He was put on the air as well and argued with Ham about morality, which Ham said atheists cannot have because they don't have an objective source for it. I found this an odd position to have for someone who had just lied to an audience of Christians—and at least two atheists— live on the air.

I immediately tweeted to Ham a screenshot of the job posting to which I had just been told was a job for AiG, not the Ark Encounter—strange, since the posting clearly said "Ark Encounter" in the description multiple times. I knew Ham was lying, and I knew I needed to stop him. I knew the job would be too big to do on my own, however, so I decided to get help. But first, I thought I would test the waters with the job opening. A reader of my blog who wishes to remain anonymous and who happened to be qualified for the CAD position applied for the job. This person, whom I'll call JM, received a letter back asking him to sign all the statements of faith previously mentioned to proceed with the application process. The discrimination could not have been clearer.

I contacted Rob Boston,[7] director of communications for Americans United for the Separation of Church and State (AU). I had seen Rob speak at an American Humanist Association conference about two years before in my hometown of San Diego and knew if anyone could help, he could. I sent him links to all of my relevant articles and screenshots of the job posting and asked what could be done. He replied fairly quickly, letting me know all the information I provided had been passed on to the legal team at AU.

AU liked what I had found and decided it was time to take action. They drafted a letter to the governor of Kentucky, Steve Beshear, and the Kentucky Tourism Development Finance Authority. In the letter, AU stated, "Per the required Statement of Faith, an applicant must profess, inter alia, that homosexuality is a sin on par with bestiality and incest, that the earth is only 6,000 years old, and that the bible is literally true in order to be considered for the job. . . . Ark Encounter's participation in the tax incentive program would compel taxpayers in the state to support both religious discrimination and a religious ministry."[8]

The AU letter went on to directly reference my articles and the work JM put into exposing the employment violation:

Ark Encounter has, however, already begun turning away the diverse citizens of Kentucky, hiring only from a particular religious sect. See also Dan Arel, The Dishonesty Continues from Ken Ham and Answers in Genesis, Danthropology, August 13, 2014, http://www.patheos.com/blogs/danthropology/2014/08/thedishonesty-continues-from-ken-ham-and-answers-in-genesis/. This is inconsistent with the universal economic good that the tourism tax incentive program is meant to promote and with the deal Ark Encounter earlier struck with the State of Kentucky. Any contrary argument—for example, that it is Answers in Genesis rather than Ark Encounter that is discriminating on the basis of religion—is necessarily formalistic at the expense of the obvious intent of Ark Encounter's prior agreement with the State. While there have always been doubts as to the propriety and legality of Ark Encounter's participation in the tourism tax incentive program, the organization has by its recent actions demonstrated that it is unsuited to participate by any measure.

With the letter sent, we waited for a reply. As I had learned from my years in activism, however, I would not wait quietly. I followed AiG and Ham's actions every single day. I wrote articles about evolution, creationism, and even Ham's affiliation with a known white supremacist who happened to donate a cool dinosaur fossil to the Creation Museum. When you are waiting for a reply from the government, or are at a standstill with one aspect of a cause, you have to keep the pressure on. I had become something of a go-to for comment on all things related to Ken Ham, so I used that additional exposure to discredit his work and to call attention to the real damage he caused to children by pushing his creation myth. I also posted regular updates for readers on the happenings around the Ark Encounter project so that they would know someone was still working hard against it.

By now, with the letter from AU making its rounds in the media, almost every major news source had picked up the story about AiG's discriminatory practice. The pressure was on to act. I wrote a really fun article for *American Atheist* magazine called "Preferring Fear to Understanding" that really set Ham off.[9] In the article, I made reference to an episode of *Cosmos* in which the the story of the Ark is compared to the Epic of Gilgamesh, from which the Ark myth is clearly derived.

In the episode entitled "The Immortals," [Neil deGrasse] Tyson explains the origins of the human drive to tell and then later write stories. He recounts the Epic of Gilgamesh, the tale of a man who built a massive ark to protect two of every kind of animal from an impending flood. The flood ends when a dove is released from the ark and returns with a branch in its beak. Anyone

*familiar with Judeo-Christian myth knows that this is
also the story of Noah's Ark. The only difference is that
the Epic of Gilgamesh is thousands of years older than
the Noah story.*

I knew my activism against the Ark Encounter might help prevent tax dollars from going to it, but that ultimately I could not stop the park from being built. However, I also knew I would do everything within my power to educate the public about the origins of the myth and the harm done by teaching children that the story of Noah and the Ark was true. Ham, by publishing my aforementioned article on his own blog along with his response, helped expand my reach to creationists by putting my name and words into the households of his creationist readers. In that sense, I had managed to get him to do some of my work for me. While I doubt this or other articles I wrote changed any minds on the spot, I like to think that maybe they planted even the smallest seeds of doubt in a few heads.

Given the weakness of Ham's responses to my articles, Ham may have inadvertently planted a few seeds of his own in some minds. For example, in response to my piece on the similarities between these two ancient flood stories, he wrote:

*Now, obviously atheists don't believe the Bible's account
of Noah's Flood, but to equate the biblical account*

> *with the Gilgamesh epic displays an ignorance of both. For example, the animal-gathering activities in the Gilgamesh flood legend were quite vague. The Gilgamesh story doesn't refer to pairs of animals or the reason for gathering them. But God's Word makes it clear that God sent a worldwide Flood as a judgment for the overwhelming, widespread wickedness of that time. But in grace, God spared Noah's family and representatives of all the kinds of air-breathing land animals to repopulate the earth.*

Basically, Ham argues that because there are some minor differences between the two stories, and because the Noah's Ark story gives more detail about how the animals got onto the boat, the biblical story is true and that's that. In effect, he hopes his readers are as gullible as he is.

For me, this is a big part of activism in the secular world. You have to hold believers accountable to their claims and force them to defend their beliefs when they want to push them on the public, especially when they want to teach their myths to children as solid facts. They tend to struggle to defend their beliefs because they are usually indoctrinated themselves or because they are pushing their beliefs for profit, such as in the case of megachurch pastors. These con artists care little for the gospel and care only about the money they can make by preaching it. You expose their ignorance when you demand they defend their claims. If they claim something is true, the onus is on them to prove it. Saying simply that "this story is slightly different" explains nothing and shows that Ham was probably very unfamiliar with the original myth to begin with.

Yet, without fail, the second you start holding believers accountable for their beliefs or questioning their power to dictate how the rest of us should live our lives, you are labeled a hateful anti-Christian. The more pressure I put on Ham, for example, the more he would argue that I was persecuting him for his religious beliefs and charge that I was anti-Christian. He even posted about me on Facebook, saying, "No, his hatred for Christianity does not come through at all in the words he uses—unless you actually read them!"[10]

The Christian persecution complex is not something unique to Ham and is used in almost all Christian arguments when Christians find out they are not getting their way. As a secular activist, this is something you will need to get used to, so it's necessary to discuss its variations here. When the Supreme Court legalized same-sex marriage in 2015, for example, the Christian Right screamed the ruling was an attack on religious liberty. Never, at least in my own lifetime, have I seen such whining about losing the right to discriminate. Some Christians even cried that they were now living through one of their toughest times in history, comparing their condition to Jews in Nazi Germany. It was a fantastic display of a total lack of self-awareness.

Of course, the only liberty they lost was the ability to persecute and oppress homosexuals. I even had a family member tell me he was sick of Christians being persecuted because he was being "forced" to be accepting of transgender people. When Christians lose cases to close women's health clinics that provide abortion services, they tell you this is a loss of religious liberty, even though they never have to step inside one of these clinics if they choose not to.

After the November 2015 Planned Parenthood shooting by Christian terrorist Robert L. Dear in which three people were killed, some conservative politicians did nothing more than offer "thoughts and prayers" on Twitter. As a result, they received a great deal of backlash for refusing to act politically to curb the rise of gun violence and mass shootings. This backlash quickly became known as "prayer shaming," and the Christian Right accused anyone who suggested that politicians should change laws rather than pray of persecuting the religious for their beliefs.

Even the lawsuit filed by American Atheists against the 9/11 Museum due to its inclusion of a Christian cross was framed as a loss of religious liberty. The Christian Right lost its mind, charging persecution by atheists. As I described earlier, however, the demand from American Atheists was simple and fair: either include atheists as well or include no one.

The Christian persecution complex is even now featured in Hollywood, with movies like *God's Not Dead*, in which an atheist philosophy professor forces a student to either sign a paper declaring God is dead or enter into a debate with the professor. Of course, the movie ends with the professor admitting that he hates God and that he blames God for the death of his mother, an ending that pushes the Christian belief that atheists are just mad at God. If that's not on the nose enough, yes, there is even a movie titled *Persecution*, in which a pastor is framed for murder by the government because of his work to stop a bill that would destroy freedom.

YouTube videos have been released with Catholics mimicking the homosexual-positive "It Gets Better" videos. In the Catholic version, Catholics tell stories about being shamed and laughed at for being against same-sex marriage and describe how they feel unsafe being who they are. Yes, they actually try to compare the "struggles" they face as bigots with the struggles faced by those who are actually oppressed and even murdered for being born homosexual. That's how far this persecution complex has gone.

The sick irony is that in North Korea and countries throughout the Middle East, Christians are being persecuted, even beheaded, and yet the Christian Right does nothing for them and instead cries for hours about same-sex marriage and bodily autonomy! Benjamin Dixon, a *Patheos* blogger, wrote to his fellow Christians that this persecution complex is embarrassing because it "would appear that you can't even endure what essentially amounts to someone no longer being the popular girl in school."[11]

Fox News mouthpiece Todd Starnes had the audacity to go on the air and tell the falsified story of Air Force Sergeant Phillip Monk,[12] who tried to convince the world he had been relieved of duty after siding with an instructor who voiced his religious objections to homosexuality to his openly gay commander. The story was totally false. Monk had not been terminated; his assignment simply ended.[13] Even so, Starnes had Monk on his show, feeding further this persecution complex. "Christians have to go into the closet," Monk told Starnes. "We are being robbed of our dignity and respect. We can't be who we are." Starnes added, "In essence, Christians are trading places with homosexuals."

Taking the place of homosexuals? Homosexuals, up until the recent Supreme Court ruling, were not allowed to be married in many states, not permitted spousal rights to hospital visits, and not legally able to adopt. Yet today, because Christians cannot continue to persecute and discriminate against homosexuals, they are somehow the new homosexual?

Politicians such as Republican Senator James Lankford of Oklahoma tell Christians they must hide their beliefs for fear of persecution—a strange sentiment when Christians are the overwhelming majority of the country. You literally cannot walk outside in the United States and not bump into a Christian. I have a "Good Without a God" sticker on my car and it gets negative notes left on it regularly, yet I am betting those with Christian "Not of This World" stickers do not deal with similar antagonism. But back to Lankford's lunacy.

"We have an undercurrent of conversations happening in the country, where there's become a redefinition of the term 'religious liberty,'" Lankford said in a November 2015 talk to the Family Research Council. "Is this a term that has the same meaning as we use it out in the common vernacular? And I would tell you, across the country and multiple places that I've visited, 'no' is the correct answer. This term is attempting to be redefined by our culture to say if you're for religious liberty, then you're hatred [sic] towards other people, you're exclusive, you're divisive, you're a person who needs to be isolated because you're for religious liberty. . . . I would say to you, people of faith in the workplace and in public settings have become the new individuals that are targeted towards 'don't ask, don't tell.'"

Texas Senator Ted Cruz has similarly warned of Christian persecution, suggesting that Christians could be imprisoned for their beliefs: "If you think your faith is safe, next may be you. Next may be me. Next may be your pastor who preaches the Word from the pulpit. Next might be your sister or brother or mom who volunteers at the pregnancy crisis center."

Of course Ken Ham regularly gets in on the action. A public park in Delaware erected a large Noah's Ark play area. Once Americans United got involved, the city removed it. Ham was not happy as you can imagine and took to his blog:

> *This clearly shows their agenda—to keep any mention of God or Christianity out of the public arena. Despite our Christian heritage in America, AU is trying to obliterate all signs of God from our culture. As atheist groups like AU continue to be vocal and win victories like this one, we can only expect religious freedom to continue to decrease. We need to understand that when an atheist group like this has a Christian display/ message removed, they have successfully removed the Christian religion and are now imposing their religion of atheism on the culture.*[14]

It is pretty obvious to anyone paying attention that no religious freedom was lost here. Biblical displays are welcome on any private property or private park that will have them, but for a government-funded park to display anything promoting one religion or any religion for that matter is a clear violation of the establishment clause—such a violation is, in fact, a decrease in religious freedom.

These are the same arguments we have every year around Christmas when nativity scenes start to pop up on government land and atheist or secular groups ask for equal space to display something of their own. In those cases in which atheists get permission to add a secular display, their displays are often targeted by vandals—vandals doing the Lord's work, presumably. Like the Bible says, "Vandalize things you disagree with"—at least, I am sure that line's in there, because otherwise Christians would never intentionally destroy someone else's property or do anything illegal, right?

The fear Christian leaders and politicians drive into the hearts of believers is almost unreal. It is no wonder atheists and secularists are so distrusted in the United States. Christian leaders are telling their flocks on a daily basis that we are after them and will imprison them for their bigotry. And, of course, if you dare question them or call them out for this persecution complex, you are, as Ham accuses me, anti-Christian. This only adds to their sense of persecution. As they perceive it, their "freedom" to oppress people is gone, and they are hated to boot. Still, they endure because their faith is so important.

Regardless of what Ham writes about me, I know I am not anti-Christian. I am against taxpayer dollars being used to proselytize to children under the guise of a theme park. I am against schools losing much-needed money to a theme park that celebrates the mass genocide of millions, myth or not.

After Americans United sent its letter to the governor of Kentucky, the persecution complex went into full swing. Ham blogged that "anti-Christian groups and the secular media have launched a massive propaganda war (continuing to this day) in their attempt to undermine the Ark Encounter."

This was because the Commonwealth of Kentucky started to question its decision to give the park taxpayer money. "We expect all of the companies that get tax incentives to obey the law," said Gil Lawson, communications director for the Kentucky Tourism, Arts and Heritage Cabinet. It seemed obvious that the park was not planning to obey the law. Thus, Answers in Genesis needed to go on the offense, and fast. "We're hoping the state takes a hard look at their position, and changes their position so it doesn't go further than this," said AiG Executive President Mike Zovath. He argued that the state would "violate the organization's First Amendment and state constitutional rights" if it rejected the application.

Ham used this persecution complex myth to his advantage in his fundraising pitches. He wrote to donors that because of the pressure of "liberal newspapers" on the local government, "our freedom of speech and freedom of religion with this outreach are now under attack."[15] He went as far as to claim that the state sent him a letter criticizing the park for "having an evangelistic purpose and possibly hiring Ark staff who agree with our Christian faith."

No one ever asked Ham to change his message. Rather, he was simply told that if he wanted taxpayer money, then he had to follow the law. Ham chose to open the Ark Encounter as a for-profit business, for which he must adhere to federal and state laws. Yet, by his own words, Ham appears to believe those laws do not apply because of his Christian faith. He was never asking to be treated equally; he was asking for religious privilege. He wanted to be treated as if he and his organization were above the law.

His attitude is no different than the attitude of countless others who confuse challenges to their religious privilege with genuine persecution. Recall how Juan Mendez was attacked for daring to ask everyone to come together as humans in his invocation. The very omission of a Christian prayer in a government setting was seen as an attack on Christianity, even though he never mentioned Christianity even once. Those who howled persecution never complained that his secular invocation also didn't mention Allah or Buddha. The reality is they don't care about any other religion; they care only about their specific privilege that they believe is rightfully theirs.

As the Christian Right loses more and more ground—and as secular activism grows in strength, size, and effectiveness—we can expect the Christian persecution complex to increase. As Christians get knocked off their pedestal of privilege, they will likely be told by their leaders that atheists want to round them up—to exterminate them—in order to end their religion in the United States and around the world. They know how badly they have treated and continue to treat other groups in this country, such as homosexuals, Muslims, and yes, atheists, and they fear they will be treated in the same manner.

What Christian leaders and politicians don't want their followers to understand is that atheists don't hate believers, even if we may often hate the disease that is religion, and we may want this disease cured so people can lead even better, more fulfilling lives, free of useless myths. This is quite similar to how we all hate cancer, but we do not hate cancer patients. I want to eradicate cancer, but I don't think you should eradicate those with cancer in order to do so. We can eradicate religion, through the vaccine of truth, spread vocally around the world. The cure to religion is education, not murder. Religious leaders know this and know that it sounds much less scary than the harmful rhetoric they rely on now to maintain control over their flocks.

So, currently, our job for securing a truly secular world is two-fold. We must educate people away from religious dogma, and we must also educate them on what it means to be secular. This process will not always be easy. In the interim, we will face both losses and victories, as I will explore in chapters 3 and 4.

Notes

1.   U.S. Supreme Court Opinion, *Town of Greece, New York v. Galloway et al.*, No. 12–696, argued November 6, 2013, decided May 5, 2014.

2.   American Atheists, "Atheists Condemn Arizona State Representative's Prayer 'Do-Over' after Secular Invocation," press release, May 24, 2013, http://news.atheists.org/2013/05/24/press-release-atheists-condemn-arizona-state-senators-prayer-do-over-after-secular-invocation-american-atheists-demands-lawmaker-apologize-to-all-non-christians/.

3.   Chris Stedman, "Arizona Rep. Juan Mendez: We Need Atheist Invocations," Religion News Service, May 14, 2014, http://chrisstedman.religionnews.com/2014/05/14/greece-vs-galloway-az-rep-juan-mendez-need-atheist-invocations/.

4.   Dan Arel, "Atheists Are Not Offended by a Cross, They Are Offended by Discrimination," *Huffington Post*, March 10, 2014, http://www.huffingtonpost.com/dan-arel/atheists-are-not-offended_b_4927592.html.

5.   Told you.

6.   U.S. Equal Employment Opportunity Commission, "Religious Discrimination," http://www.eeoc.gov/laws/types/religion.cfm (accessed June 24, 2016).

7. Don't call him Boston Rob.

8. Americans United for the Separation of Church and State, in its letter to Governor Steve Beshear dated August 22, 2014, https://www.au.org/files/pdf_documents/2014-08-22%20Frankfort%252c%20KY%20-%20Ark%20Park%20Religious%20Discrimination.pdf.

9. Dan Arel, "Ken Ham Has an Issue with My Latest Article for American Atheist Magazine," *Patheos*, November 4, 2014, http://www.patheos.com/blogs/danthropology/2014/11/ken-ham-has-an-issue-with-my-latest-article-for-american-atheists-magazine/.

10. Post on Ken Ham's Facebook page dated August 8, 2014, https://www.facebook.com/aigkenham/posts/798429863520705?fref=nf.

11. Benjamin Dixon, "Please Stop with the Christian Persecution Complex. You're Embarrassing the Faith," *Patheos*, July 9, 2015, http://www.patheos.com/blogs/godisnotarepublican/2015/07/please-stop-with-the-christian-persecution-complex-youre-embarrassing-the-faith/.

12. Starnes is the closest thing to a talking pig you'll ever see. He is the worst, seriously.

13. "The Persecution Complex: The Religious Right's Deceptive Rallying Cry," People for the American Way, http://www.pfaw.org/rww-in-focus/persecution-complex-religious-

right-s-deceptive-rallying-cry (accessed June 24, 2016).

14.   Ken Ham, "Another Ark Attack," Answers in Genesis, December 3, 2014, http://blogs.answersingenesis.org/blogs/ken-ham/2014/12/03/another-ark-attack.

15.   Dan Arel, "Ken Ham Claims He Is Being Attacked for Being a Christian," *Patheos*, November 29, 2014, http://www.patheos.com/blogs/danthropology/2014/11/ken-ham-claims-he-is-being-attacked-for-being-a-christian/.

3

LOSSES

Not every aspect of activism is glamorous. Sometimes we stink at it. Governments and courts often let us down. Far too often they side with the majority, or with their own personal ideologies, over clear-cut constitutional law. Too often we hear judges insert their own personal feelings into cases when their feelings have little or nothing to do with what is being argued. We see politicians take the side of their own personal religion even when they know their decision will mean the oppression of those they are supposed to represent.

These courts let us down when they decide that corporations are people and give them unlimited power to influence elections. They let us down when they uphold restrictions on women's health clinics that are wholly unconstitutional but that align with the beliefs of the judges. Politicians let us down when they spend endless weeks voting to repeal the Affordable Care Act and sit on their hands when it comes to voting to secure medical aid and assistance for 9/11 first responders. As citizens, we are used to being let down—sadly, when it comes to secular activism, the story is no different.

We don't win every battle we fight. American Atheists lost the 9/11 cross case. Today, the 9/11 Museum displays a man-made cross we are supposed to believe is a result of a miracle. They want us to believe it was created by the same guy who did nothing to stop those two planes from crashing into the World Trade Center towers—the same guy who allowed the rubble in the first place.

Some cities and towns have stood firm in saying that secularists cannot give secular invocations, and some courthouses and other government buildings freely display the Ten Commandments. The Holy Land Experience in Florida, a Jesus-based theme park, receives millions of dollars in Florida taxpayer money because of a law passed by the local government.

We don't win every fight, but we cannot stop trying to protect constitutional principles. When we lose, we dust ourselves off and do it all over again. Why? Because we know it is the right thing to do, not only for secularism but also for religious liberty. The reason these battles are so important is that they are not simply about removing Christian themes from public places; they are also about reminding the Christian Right that this is not *their* country—it is *our* country. Christians have placed themselves on a pedestal and, for generations, society has allowed them that place. They have stayed on top, unquestioned, and been allowed to make the demands they wish and buy the politicians they want, thus ensuring their place on the pedestal remains unchanged.

Well, the status quo isn't going to cut it anymore. Since 9/11 and the rise of the so-called new atheist movement, organizations like American Atheists are being taken more seriously than ever before. Atheists are becoming vocal and strident in their demand that those of all religions and no religion be treated equally in the eyes of the law. The Christian Right hates this because its leaders and constituents truly believe they are above the law. The biggest threat to them is being brought down to our level in the real world, one in which they must abide by the same laws as everyone else.[1]

They also hate that this would mean other religions would be on equal footing with theirs. They have spent years, especially since 9/11, making sure Islam is treated as lower than dirt. They fight to close mosques, stop Islamic centers from being built, and even to convince the world that President Barack Obama is a Muslim—to them, that is the ultimate insult. They cannot imagine a time or place in which they have to share equal rights with Muslims and atheists, and they will seemingly stop at nothing to make sure this never happens.

In Lincoln County, North Carolina, a humanist group fought and was granted permission to deliver a secular invocation. However, the prospect of also allowing a Muslim a similar courtesy was just too much, so the board of commissioners changed its policy altogether, stopping all invocations, both religious and secular. This is technically a win for secularism because invocations have no place in government settings, but the secular community did lose an opportunity to give an invocation to show what we are all about, if only to that local community.

In the face of losses, we must continue to make our voices heard, stand for true religious freedom, and uphold our principles. Religious groups now know that when they try to get the government to promote a certain sectarian practice, secular groups like American Atheists will be there. If a local government tries to install a Noah's Ark playground, Americans United will have something to say. If a public school teacher tries to use a Bible in the classroom or tell a student they must consider the word of God in any way, the Freedom From Religion Foundation will show up.

One ongoing fight the American Humanist Association and Americans United are involved in relates to the Pledge of Allegiance, which I wrote about in *Parenting Without God*:

The Pledge of Allegiance is a rather touchy topic in the United States. It is a common misconception among the religious that the words "under God" are an original part of the pledge. Few do the actual research to realize that those words were added in 1954. The pledge itself was written by Francis Bellamy in 1892.

Bellamy's original pledge reads as follows: "I pledge allegiance to my Flag and the Republic for which it stands, one nation indivisible, with liberty and justice for all."

It underwent many changes before 1954, but adding "under God" was not one of them. The final change before 1954 is the version we should still be saying today (I say should be, but will touch on that later): "I pledge allegiance to the flag of the United States of America, and to the Republic for which it stands, one Nation indivisible, with liberty and justice for all." . . .

I have heard of teachers who get upset when students do not recite the current version of the pledge, but do not be afraid of those teachers because you have the law and history on your side. Do not be afraid to stand up for your child's right to omit God or to not stand up at all.[2]

Removing God from the pledge is a battle I am not sure we can ever win, but if we don't fight it, we would have little ground to stand on when demanding other references to God be kept to the private domain. By fighting for the removal of God in the pledge, we are demonstrating that we are standing up for a principle—one that we will fight to have applied equally across all facets of public life.

The Hobby Lobby case represents another really tough loss for secularism. In *Burwell v. Hobby Lobby*, the Supreme Court granted the craft store the right to have a religious belief. You read that correctly: after Citizens United, corporations became people; after the Hobby Lobby case, they gained the right to hold their own religion. The entire case rested on the court's decision to interpret the idiotic Religious Freedom Restoration Act as offering protection to religious business owners who do not want to pay for health insurance that offers employees birth control methods they do not agree with.

The ruling was praised as a victory for religious freedom, but it was anything but. It removed the rights of employees' to their own religious freedom and gave all the power to corporations. Suddenly your boss has more control over your sex life than you do. Needless to say, secular and atheist groups were not pleased with the ruling.

"This is a disgrace and an indignity to Americans' right to be protected from the abuses of other people's religions," said American Atheists President David Silverman, in a press release following the ruling. "Shame on the Supreme

Court, which has effectively told Americans that if you can come up with a religious excuse, you are above the law. This is an injustice of the highest order for separation of religion and government, for equality, and for the constitutional protections guaranteed to all Americans."

"The Court has granted religious liberties to some corporations, claiming they have the same rights as citizens. What about the rights of the women, the workers? We fear the consequences of this decision on publicly traded corporations in the future," added American Atheists Managing Director Amanda Knief, a lawyer and public policy expert.[3]

The ruling carried the even scarier possibility of opening the door to other "religious freedoms" that might be used to discriminate against not only employees but also the public at large. "If employers can reject the birth-control pills for their employees by citing their religious objections to contraception, do employers also have a right to refuse serving gay couples because they abhor same-sex marriages?" asked William Greider in a piece for *The Nation*.

"A principal concern about the impact of Hobby Lobby is whether the decision will open the door for religious objections to override laws that prohibit discrimination in employment and other arenas," Alex Luchenitser wrote for *Harvard Law and Policy Review*. "Will the decision usher in a new era of inequality in which businesses have a right to refuse to hire or serve persons whose identities or conduct are condemned by the theological teachings of the businesses' owners?"

Luchenitser concluded that Congress would need to act quickly to fix this, but given that Congress has been taken over by the Religious Right, this is unlikely to happen anytime soon. "Religion should not become a trump card that allows one who professes it to hire or serve whomever they want," he wrote. "Hobby Lobby represents a step in the direction of such a retrograde society, atomized and divided by corporate theocracy. Congress should amend RFRA before any more steps are taken toward such an era of inequality."[4]

The ruling was a global embarrassment, something that has basically become par for the course from the Supreme Court in the last decade. The only ruling related to secularism they seem to have gotten right as far as I can remember is the same-sex marriage ruling.

A loss like this should not leave us feeling defeated, however. We must face a ruling like this with great resolve. We must fight to undo it and to make sure predictions like those of Luchenitser don't become a reality. When the Christian Right wins a victory like this, they feel unstoppable and try to see how far they can push their "freedom." Christian bakeries have already begun to refuse to bake cakes for same-sex weddings, and grimy pizza joints are announcing they won't cater same-sex weddings, even though no one is asking.

In a sense, it is the losses that fuel us. Of course we want to win all of these battles, but there are so many, and we are realistic by definition. Atheists must apply their critical-thinking skills to their activism. We know that change does not come overnight. We must have the courage and tenacity to work hard for it. The great abolitionist Frederick Douglass once said:

> *If there is no struggle, there is no progress. Those who profess to favor freedom, and yet depreciate agitation, are men who want crops without plowing up the ground. They want rain without thunder and lightning. They want the ocean without the awful roar of its many waters. This struggle may be a moral one; or it may be a physical one; or it may be both moral and physical; but it must be a struggle. Power concedes nothing without a demand. It never did and it never will.*[5]

Without a struggle, we can't generate change. Even if we could overcome each obstacle with a snap of the fingers, it is possible we would just get too lazy to keep going. We need to be reminded why we are fighting. Overcoming adversity gives us strength and makes the victories we get even more meaningful and encourages us to keep moving forward. I wish I could change the world overnight, but I cannot, so we must continue our fight and overcome these struggles.

I'll gladly lose a fight over a cross in a museum today to overturn an unjust law governing women's bodies tomorrow. Further, both results, in their own right, can be seen as victories. In the former case, we make our voices heard and reach more people who want to become involved; in the latter, we uphold women's bodily autonomy.

In San Diego, where I live, a Christian group installed a giant cross on public land as part of a World War II memorial and claimed the cross didn't represent Christianity. Well, a Jewish veteran took offense and sued the city, and the state, and the federal government. Secular groups became involved because the case mattered to us all. The courts did the right thing and ordered the cross removed. In response, the government sold the land to a private entity, ending the battle and ensuring that the cross remained.

This result was perhaps a loss in the broad sense of the word, because the government caved to Christian demands by selling public land, but the positive side is that disparate groups came together to demand change and challenge the Christian Right. We told them you cannot claim the cross is Christian when it benefits you and then call it secular when you want to use it on government land. Secular and Jewish organizations worked together because they had a common goal, which was to end religious discrimination. By selling the land and hurting far more Americans than it helped, however, the government once again showed that the Christian Right carries much of the power in this country. This experience offers a stark reminder of our struggle, and why we continue to fight.

It is easy to become discouraged after losses and to contemplate giving up. I can vividly remember losing battle after battle when I worked in animal rights and seeing people leave the movement depressed. I hate when I see atheists and secularists leaving for the same reasons. Losing sucks! It's not easy to deal with losing, and sometimes it can feel like you're fighting a war that you've already lost before you've even started to fight. In the United States, we are up against a giant. The Christian Right's numbers are massive. But there is hope. According to a 2015 study by the Pew Research Center, the United States is becoming less religious:

A growing share of Americans are religiously unaffiliated, including some who self-identify as atheists or agnostics as well as many who describe their religion as "nothing in particular." Altogether, the religiously unaffiliated (also called the "nones") now account for 23% of the adult population, up from 16% in 2007.[6]

The so-called nones, regardless of their belief in a personal god, are the fastest growing minority group in the

United States and the largest voting block among minority "religious" groups. This is bad news for the Christian Right, as it continues to lose its hold in government. The Pew study also reveals that atheism itself is quickly growing: "The share of Americans who say they are 'absolutely certain' that God exists has dropped eight percentage points, from 71 percent to 63 percent, since 2007, when the last comparable study was made."

As the percentage of atheists and "nones" in the country rises, the percentage of those affiliated with religion must be dropping. The study confirms this: "The percentage of adults who describe themselves as 'religiously affiliated' has shrunk six points since 2007, from 83 percent to 77 percent"; "The shares of the U.S. adult population who consider religion 'very important' to them, pray daily, and attend services at least once a month have declined between three and four percent over the last eight years."

A variety of factors explain this dramatic shift. Religion is slipping in the United States largely because the population is becoming more educated and because the Internet is readily available in most households, which is giving people access to information like never before. The landscape of the nation is quickly changing and religion has found itself unable to adapt. Meanwhile, science continues to make discoveries about the universe and our place in it. As a result, fewer and fewer people are looking to religion for answers to life's big questions.

Another major factor changing the religious landscape of the United States is age. According to another Pew study from May 2015, younger generations are less religious than older ones:

As the Millennial generation enters adulthood, its members display much lower levels of religious affiliation, including less connection with Christian churches, than older generations. Fully 36% of young Millennials (those between the ages of 18 and 24) are religiously unaffiliated, as are 34% of older Millennials (ages 25–33). And fewer than six-in-ten Millennials identify with any branch of Christianity, compared with seven-in-ten or more among older generations, including Baby Boomers and Gen-Xers. Just 16% of Millennials are Catholic, and only 11% identify with mainline Protestantism. Roughly one-in-five are evangelical Protestants.[7]

The study found that the number of adults who describe themselves as Christians has dropped nearly eight percent over the past seven years. What could cause such a drop in the Christian population of the United States? As the study states,

The drop in the Christian share of the population has been driven mainly by declines among mainline Protestants and Catholics. Each of those large religious traditions has shrunk by approximately three percentage points since 2007. The evangelical Protestant share of the U.S. population also has dipped, but at a slower rate, falling by about one percentage point since 2007.

Meanwhile, religiously unaffiliated adults have grown by 19 million (a 19.2 percent increase), bringing their estimated numbers to 56 million, as compared to 51 million Catholic adults, a drop of almost 3 million since 2007.

This means that secularism is on the rise in the United States, but it does not mean we should stop fighting and simply wait for religious influence in the public square to fade away. A fellow atheist once told me they didn't think we should focus on marriage equality because it would eventually work itself out and we could be using our energy to focus on other issues that may not. I couldn't believe the argument. Generations of same-sex couples should wait for society to catch up? That just *did not* sit well with me! Even if we knew for certain society would catch up in time, why wait? I knew we could all impact lives now and give same-sex couples the legal recognition and rights they had desperately wanted. There is no need to wait for change when we can make a difference today!

Things may be looking up, but we must not be complacent. We are going to lose some fights. If we do, we must dust ourselves off, learn from our experience, and try again. We will know we are on the side of right because we will be fighting for the disenfranchised and the oppressed. We will be defending religious liberty on all fronts, not just for the freedoms that interest or directly benefit us. We must not find ourselves discouraged; others are counting on us. Those of us who are in a position to be able to discuss these issues openly, to write books about them and debate them, can use our privilege to set wrongs right. We should see it as an honor to do so and use the challenges ahead as a source of inspiration to keep going.

But enough talk about losses. Let's talk about the big wins.

Notes

1. This is pointed out perfectly in David Silverman's book *Fighting God: An Atheist Manifesto for a Religious World* (New York: Thomas Dunne, 2016).

2. Dan Arel, *Parenting Without God: How to Raise Moral, Ethical and Intelligent Children, Free from Religious Dogma* (Durham, NC: Pitchstone Publishing, 2015).

3. American Atheists, "Atheists Decry Court's Grant of Religious Rights to Corporations in Hobby Lobby," press

release, June 30, 2014, http://news.atheists.org/2014/06/30/atheists-decry-courts-grant-of-religious-rights-to-corporations-in-hobby-lobby/.

4. Alex J. Luchenitser, "AU Attorney Dissects Hobby Lobby Ruling for Harvard Law & Policy Review," *Church & State*, May 2105, https://www.au.org/church-state/may-2015-church-state/people-events/au-attorney-dissects-hobby-lobby-ruling-for-harvard.

5. Douglass, Frederick, "No Struggle, No Progress," 1857.

6. "U.S. Public Becoming Less Religious," Pew Research Center, November 3, 2015, http://www.pewforum.org/2015/11/03/u-s-public-becoming-less-religious/.

7. "America's Changing Religious Landscape," Pew Research Center, May 12, 2015, http://www.pewforum.org/2015/05/12/americas-changing-religious-landscape/.

4

VICTORIES

"Let us rise each morning, and strive each day, to do only that which brings happiness and joy to others, and avoid doing things that cause others hurt and pain," declared Ted Utchen on a Monday night in Wheaton, Illinois, during his secular invocation in front of the Wheaton City Council.[1] "Let us use our minds and our reason to encourage behavior based on the mutuality and reciprocity inherent in human relationships, and let us always respect the dignity and worth of each other." He continued, "And let us, above all, love one another, not to obtain rewards for ourselves now or hereafter or to avoid punishment, but rather always to bring each other contentment and peace. So be it."

Utchen approached the Wheaton City Council and asked to deliver the invocation after he heard the call to action from those like Arizona State Representative Juan Mendez. His simple act made national headlines. His message was "devoid of mentions of a higher power," reported Billy Hallowell for *The Blaze*, a Christian Right publication.

Utchen's message wasn't antireligious and really shouldn't have been news at all. Yet, for some reason, it is national news to not mention God in a secular government meeting these days. This of course makes the work of ensuring we do deliver such invocations just that much more important. Thankfully, there are activists out there doing just that.

In Longwood, Florida, U.S. Army veteran Loren Kahle demanded to be heard, and she was. On September 10, 2015, the eve of the fourteenth anniversary of the 9/11 attacks, Kahle addressed the City Commission.

> *Tonight is the eve of one of the most important dates in American history. 9/11 will forever remind us how important it is to set aside differences and unify under a common purpose. We were unified then with a common vision and by our unique American spirit. That spirit continues to bring all people together and continues to make our country great.*[2]

In her secular invocation, she called for principles of inclusion in our society, saying, "By adhering to principles of inclusion, we ensure respect for everyone, even those from our community who are not present this evening, regardless of differences and especially regardless of beliefs. Because of that diversity, it is not possible for one person to speak in a manner appropriate for all."

Such moments are happening all over the country. Some battles are still being fought, and some cities, towns, and states are still saying no, but they are losing and they are realizing the fight is not worth it. I dare someone to find anything offensive in any of the secular invocations being read around the world. They are a call for togetherness and inclusion that is not based on belief but on pure human decency. It is humanism in action.

Other such victories in the secular movement are not hard to find. In Florida, for example, a wonderful monument to secular principles and values today sits outside the Bradford County Courthouse, thanks to efforts by American Atheists and other secular activists. They initially demanded the removal of a Ten Commandments monument outside the courthouse, but the county refused and instead chose to make the space available to any group wishing to install a monument.

In 2015 California joined Oregon by passing a death-with-dignity law, giving those suffering from terminal illness control over their lives and deaths—two things the Christian Right believes it should have control over. States have also begun to pass laws that grant protection to LGBTQ individuals, ensuring they cannot be legally discriminated against.

As activists helped secure these and other victories, my fight against Ken Ham's Ark Encounter tax incentive had become a waiting game. Ham continued to promote the park and talk about how much he was being persecuted, and job postings still existed that stated that employees must sign a statement of faith. He and his cronies were on a media blitz, finding any outlet they could that would let them tell only their side of the story. They painted a picture of evil secularists and atheists who hated Christianity so much they would destroy a man's dream to build a boat in the middle of a field.

Ham was very sure of himself. In an extremely cocky move, he took out a huge billboard near the park site that read, "To Our Intolerant Liberal Friends: THANK GOD YOU CAN'T SINK THIS SHIP." I guess no one told Ham how ships work, but you can't actually sink a landlocked boat, hundreds of miles from shore. But more importantly, the entire billboard missed the whole point, highlighting further Ham's persecution complex. No one was trying to sink his ship; we just didn't want taxpayers paying for the useless thing to be built. This is a huge difference. The entire campaign has been about ending unconstitutional tax subsidies and incentives, not stopping construction. You didn't see any atheist activist chaining themselves to trees to stop the destruction of a beautiful field to build a monument to genocide. Wait . . . perhaps we missed an opportunity there! Oh, well.

Yet, almost as though there were a God, Ham's cockiness was about to come back and bite him square in the ass, because a letter had been mailed to his lawyers from the Kentucky governor's office, and its contents could easily sink his ship. On December 10, 2014, I wrote one of the most gratifying headlines of my entire life: "Ken Ham's Ark Encounter Loses Tax Incentive."[3] It happened! The state reversed its decision to give the park an $18 million tax incentive and unraveled all the work Ham and his cronies had done up to that point.

"State tourism tax incentives cannot be used to fund religious indoctrination or otherwise be used to advance religion," Tourism Secretary Bob Stewart wrote in the letter sent to Ham's attorney. "The use of state incentives in this way violates the separation of church and state provisions of the Constitution and is, therefore, impermissible."

Even Governor Beshear, a cheerleader for the park, spoke out against its illegal practices in a statement: "While the leaders of the Ark Encounter had previously agreed not to discriminate in hiring based on religion, they now refuse to make that commitment and it has become apparent that they do intend to use religious beliefs as a litmus test for hiring decisions."

Americans United joined me in celebrating the news, issuing a statement of its own saying the park should never have been considered in the first place. "This project was never a good candidate for public funding," said the Rev. Barry W. Lynn, executive director of Americans United. "Its purpose is to promote fundamentalist Christianity, and it should be funded with private contributions from believers."

And just for good measure, Americans United posted a billboard of its own on its website that read, "Looks Like We Sunk Your Ship."

The hard work had paid off and secularism was being recognized. No one said Ham could not build his park. No one said he could not make it as Christian as he wanted. All that anyone said or has argued was that state funds cannot be used if this mission of his comes at the cost of discrimination. Of course, Ark Encounter officials did not see it this way.

Ham quickly threatened the state with a lawsuit for religious discrimination, claiming that the state knew all along that the park was religiously themed and that it was just now caving to the demands of atheists to stop its funding—again missing the point that it was the discrimination, not the theme, in question here.

"Our construction has already begun at the Williamstown, Kentucky, site, and it must proceed. We are fully prepared to defend our fundamental rights in court if necessary, as this issue is of huge importance, not only to us but to every religious organization," wrote Ham on his blog before saying that multiple law firms had agreed to take his case.

"The legal question here has already been answered unequivocally by the courts," said Mike Johnson, chief counsel of Freedom Guard, one of the firms that agreed to represent Answers in Genesis. "No state is allowed to treat religious organizations less favorably than other organizations who seek to avail themselves of a facially neutral economic incentive program. Just because some state officials may not agree with the message of a Christian organization does not mean that organization and its member can be censored or treated as second-class citizens."

These and other such statements failed to mention the real reason why Answers in Genesis lost the tax incentive. They kept claiming over and over again it was unjust because of their religious beliefs, but it had nothing to do with that and everything to do with the fact that they were discriminating against potential employees.

It wasn't long before Johnson was invited onto Fox News to defend his client. Johnson, after first calling the news "tragic," blamed atheist groups for the political pressure that led to the state's decision. He then called the reversal of the tax incentive "unlawful" and said they would likely bring their case to court. When asked how the reversal was unlawful, Johnson said that the state grants these tax incentives to all kinds of businesses but only reversed the decision when the state realized the Ark Encounter would have a "religious overtone."

From the beginning, the project was referred to as a Noah's Ark theme park—the religious undertones go without saying and came as a surprise to absolutely no one. Johnson did not once mention that the real reason they lost the incentive was because of employment discrimination.

The Fox News host then asked if the charge that someone would have to be Christian to work for the park was true. To this, Johnson answered, "Well, yeah, but that's not unlike any other religious organization in the country." He continued to argue that state and federal laws allow such hiring preference for religious organizations and stated that reversing the tax incentive based on their hiring preferences is unlawful. The host then asked Johnson if Ken Ham would be willing to hire non-Christians, and Johnson said no, because it would "change their identity."

The Fox host almost seemed to be sticking it to Johnson by asking a few tough questions, but of course, by the end of the segment, he was telling people to go to the ark site and donate money to make up for the lost tax incentive. Fox News failed to do its job as a news organization by failing to press Johnson further on these issues; instead, it acted as a Christian news organization and encouraged Christians to donate to help complete the project. True ethics in journalism over there.

The religious persecution circus act did not stop there. Mark Looey, AiG's COO, submitted an op-ed to the *Louisville*

Courier-Journal, which the newspaper apparently rejected, furthering the cries of persecution. The piece ended up being shared instead on the AiG website. In the failed op-ed, Looey wrote:

> *It is interesting to note that the state and activist secular groups can point to no specific law or statute that would deny a religious organization like AiG or Ark Encounter the right to hire staff members who agree with its mission. Indeed, why should we give in to the state's demand and give up our rights to hire people of faith? Nobody seems to want to force the group American Atheists to hire Christians (and we do not advocate it).*

When I first read this I rolled over laughing at the sheer ignorance of the statement. You don't have to look very hard to find the specific laws that Looey claims do not exist. In fact, I've already quoted them in this very book! Further, his gripe about American Atheists misses the point entirely. American Atheists, like the Ark Encounter, is bound by the 1964 Civil Rights Act. American Atheists does not have a discriminatory hiring practice in place and, as the law dictates, the organization doesn't ask employees about their religious beliefs. The Ark Encounter does.

Ham had been asked numerous times about the nearly $25 million being raised to build the park and whether the money could be used for more beneficial charitable causes, such as feeding or clothing the homeless. Well, Ham, of course, always had a ready response to this, saying that building the Ark Encounter was actually more important than feeding the homeless.

"Nearly every time I post an update on the exciting Ark Encounter project, there seem to be those habitual complainers who claim the money should be spent on the poor instead and not be 'wasted' this way," Ham wrote on his AiG blog. "The Ark project (like the Creation Museum) will in a professional, powerful, and gracious way present the truth of God's Word and the Gospel. Sadly, even some people claiming to be Christians complain about the Ark project and that the money should be given to the poor instead. Such people either don't understand or don't seem to care about the millions who will be reached with the most important food in the universe— the spiritual food of the saving Gospel—the very message that their eternal life depends on."

You're probably reading that over and over trying to figure out whether he is truly that unaware of how stupid that response sounds. Imagine the mindset of a human being who thinks building a theme park is more important than feeding the homeless. The number of homeless people who die on the streets is staggering, yet Ham believes they will have the money to come to his park and have their lives changed? He can't be serious.

Look, I am a Disneyland pass holder. My family visits the park over ten times per year, and I would personally tear the park down if it meant we could eliminate homelessness. Yet, Ham believes by preaching to the tens of people who will visit his park that he will do more good than if he instead provided safe shelter and a hot meal to the homeless. That, ladies and gentlemen, is the best example of this man's moral compass, or lack thereof, that I can give.

Rather than put their tails between their legs and walk away, Ken Ham and his colleagues doubled down on stupid, as did at least one of the project's "celebrity" supporters. Bristol Palin, the overly fertile antisex advocate and daughter of failed politician Sarah Palin, wrote on her blog that "Answers in Genesis won't be approved for the program unless they agree to hire people who aren't Christians and unless the exhibit doesn't talk about Christianity."[4] I don't remember that stipulation in the state's letter. But to really bring it home, Palin added this gem, "I just get so sick of hearing about the 'separation of church and state.' Because it usually means the state is pushing Christians around." I'll just leave that there for your personal enjoyment. Don't say I never gave you anything.

As bad as it should have made me feel, watching them flail around in this way was proof to me that what we were doing was working. The fact they could not argue their case honestly meant they knew just how dishonest and unlawful it was. They were forced to create their own narrative of religious persecution to avoid having to have an honest discussion about religious freedom, even claiming that religious freedom is "increasingly granted to the secular religion, but not Christianity."[5] They would also likely claim that state and federal laws inside a secular country do not apply to Christians, but to do this, they would first have to admit they live in a secular country, something they refuse to do. Ham, an Australian immigrant to the United States, is dead set on the belief that he moved to a Christian nation. He probably should have Googled that first.

The victory was ours, but the fight was far from over. Ham could not accept his loss and soon filed suit. "Our organization spent many months attempting to reason with state officials so that this lawsuit would not be necessary," Ham said in a video statement. "However, the state was so insistent on treating our religious entity as a second-class citizen that we were simply left with no alternative but to proceed to court. This is the latest example of increasing government hostility towards religion in America, and it's certainly among the most blatant."

The irony of Ham complaining about being a second-class citizen when he writes against same-sex marriage and promotes conversion therapy is the pure definition of irony. Hell, the guy still writes marriage in quotes when it comes to same-sex marriage. Sorry, back to his boat.

In a press release announcing the lawsuit, AiG again failed to mention the employment discrimination, instead playing on the religious message of the park.

> *Although the sales tax rebate program is available equally to all qualifying tourist attractions seeking to build in the state, AiG President Ken Ham observed that "AiG's application was rejected solely because of our religious identity and the biblical messages we will present at our future life-size Noah's Ark." Ham also noted that AIG's "lawsuit details how this action by Kentucky officials, including Gov. Steve Beshear [named as a defendant], violates federal and state law and undermines our constitutionally guaranteed religious freedom. It amounts to unlawful viewpoint discrimination against our Christian faith."[6]*

The lawsuit itself states that "by wrongfully excluding them [Ark Encounter] from participation in the Kentucky Tourism Development Program. Plaintiffs are denied access to this tourism incentive program because of who they are, what they believe, and how they express their beliefs, in flagrant disregard of their constitutional and statutory rights." I couldn't help but think this case made a mockery of our justice system. How could something so dishonest make it to a courtroom?

At this point, the story took another unexpected twist. Since the state had previously granted the park preliminary approval for the tax incentives, it had ordered a full report on the attendance projections for the park. AiG had earlier commissioned its own study and didn't understand why that was not good enough, but the state required a third-party assessment from a firm of its own choosing.

The AiG report, issued by America's Research Group (ARG), said the park would receive roughly 1.6 million visitors in the first year. Ham boasted time and time again that the park would receive around 2 million visitors. ARG even suggested that the Creation Museum would benefit by seeing a corresponding increase in visits. The state, however, contracted Hunden Strategic Partners to do the research. Hunden estimated the park would receive roughly 325,000 visitors in the first year, with a peak attendance in the third year around 425,000, declining to 275,000 after that. That is a rather large discrepancy, and there is little reason to believe Ark Encounter officials believed the initial estimates they passed on to state officials. As a point of comparison, the Creation Museum had never reached its own attendance goals up to that point.

"The Hunden Report adds more evidence that the Commonwealth of Kentucky made the correct decision in rejecting the Ark Encounter application for tax incentives," commented Ed Hensley, treasurer of the Kentucky Secular Society and co-organizer of the Freedom From Religion Foundation's Kentucky chapter. "Ken Ham, Ark Encounter, and Answers in Genesis are currently threatening to sue the Commonwealth for the right to have tax-supported religious discrimination in employment. We should consider the contrasting claims of the Hunden report while evaluating their threats."

But why the discrepancy? How could ARG come up with a number so drastically different from the one Hunden determined? Well, a bit more digging revealed that ARG is owned by Britt Beemer, and Mr. Beemer happens to be the coauthor of a book with Ken Ham.

First, this presents a major conflict of interest with the study. Ham has a working relationship and seemingly a personal relationship with the man who runs ARG. If Beemer simply helped with research for the book, as Ham claimed in a later blog post,[7] he would cite that research inside the book, not put Beemer's name on the cover.

Second, ARG, "a full-service consumer research firm which conducts national consumer surveys and strategic consulting,"[8] is perhaps not the best source for such a study to begin with. Nowhere on its website does it allude to the fact that it has the needed expertise or experience for such a large-scale report—specifically, one that involves studying the economic and fiscal impact of a tourism attraction.

If you visit the website of Hunden Strategic Partners, meanwhile, you see they are well trained and experienced in such assessments:

> *Whether you represent a public agency, tourism bureau, lending institution or a private developer, Hunden Strategic Partners provides you confidence and results via the integrity of our feasibility studies, economic and fiscal impact analyses, development strategy, solicitation processes, and related services.*[9]

So, no, no one should take the ARG report seriously. The firm is not only likely underqualified—if not unqualified—to conduct such a study, but it's also owned by a man with direct personal ties to Ken Ham, thus raising questions about neutrality. No one wants to upset their friends.

Although the trail of lies and dishonesty leading to the Ark Encounter project continued to grow, construction continued as planned. The state may have balked in its support, but the city hadn't. In a 2012 Memorandum of Agreement, the city of Williamstown, Kentucky approved $62 million in funding for Ark Encounter, LLC. The agreement says that over a thirty-year period, 75 percent of Ark Encounter's real estate taxes would go toward repayment of its interest-free tax incentive financing.

That's right, 75 percent of the real estate taxes to be paid by the Ark Encounter will go back to paying off a bond instead of going into area schools or roads. And never mind the failing healthcare system in the state, which will not participate fully in the Medicare expansion under the Affordable Care Act thanks to the newly elected Republican governor. No, instead the money will go toward propping up a massive, useless boat.[10]

The city's documents outline other incentives:

$175,000 would be given to Ark Encounter to reimburse the amount they felt the property was overvalued.

$19,000 would go to Ark Encounter's real estate agent, representing 2% of the total purchase price of the land.

98 acres of Grant County land would be sold to Ark Encounter for $1 (yes, one dollar).[11]

In short, the city of Williamstown is doing a number on taxpayers. I won't rest until this issue is resolved properly.

While Ham's lawsuit continued to move forward, I received some good personal news related to my Ark Encounter work. On April 3, 2015, I was at a friend's house watching a hockey game as the American Atheists annual convention took place in Memphis, Tennessee, an event I was very sad to miss. Suddenly, my phone exploded with text messages from people offering their congratulations, and I had no idea why.

I quickly learned that American Atheists had just given me their 2014 First Amendment Award, citing my "investigative journalism exposing religious discrimination." I was floored. I immediately emailed Rob Boston at Americans United, because, in my mind, they had won this award with me. They had taken my initial research to the next level. Together, we had done it—we had potentially saved taxpayers millions of dollars. I never set out to win awards for what I was doing. I wanted to do the right thing, and even if no one ever said thank you, I would continue doing what I did. However, for an organization as big as American Atheists to take note meant the world to me and inspired me to keep going and keep fighting. As an activist, when you feel totally alone, know that people are watching, people are cheering for you, and people want you to succeed.

I don't tell you this story about the Ark Encounter and my award to brag (well, not that much at least), but because I want it to inspire you. It still inspires me and reminds me that I can do great things. I was nothing but a guy sitting behind a keyboard who saw an issue and decided I would take action and I would do something about it.

I have no doubt that those of you reading this now are also capable of doing the same thing, if not even greater things. I am not special and I don't have a gift that you don't have. I had the will to make a difference and, by picking up this book, you do too. The fight against the Christian Right is not going to be won without you and me. It can't be won without us. The national groups need our support, whether we sit behind a keyboard, dig into our pockets, or put our boots on the ground and demand action.

Too much activism these days has become traveling to Washington, DC, on a Saturday when the Capitol is empty, milling around demanding change, and going home wondering why nothing was accomplished. We need to bring back mass protests, both literally and figuratively, as we are seeing now in the Black Lives Matter protests that started in 2015. We need to be active and we need to be out there in numbers demanding that our voices be heard—demanding an end to religious privilege in our society. We cannot sit by and let the Christian establishment do as it pleases.

If that means you march in the streets, awesome. If that means you write a blog or articles for your local paper, fantastic. If that means you donate money to secular organizations, thank you! Your activism can come in so many different forms, but don't stop being an activist. Find what works for you and demand change. Fight for change! Don't wait for someone else to do it for you, because that action might not ever come. What happens if we all sit around looking at each other wondering when someone is going to finally have the guts to do what needs to be done? I'll tell you what happens: nothing happens, and when nothing happens, we all lose.

Unfortunately, as I have learned, even our victories are not always as simple as they first seem. Sometimes, even after everything goes right, someone comes along and messes it all up.

On January 25, 2016, Judge Greg Van Tatenhove of the U.S. District Court for the Eastern District of Kentucky issued an injunction against the Commonwealth of Kentucky for blocking the Ark Encounter from participating in the Kentucky Tourism Development Program. The federal court found "that the Commonwealth's exclusion of AiG from participating in the program for the reasons stated—i.e., on the basis of AiG's religious beliefs, purpose, mission, message, or conduct, is a violation of AiG's rights under the First Amendment to the federal Constitution."

In the ruling, the judge declared that AiG may "utilize any Title VII exception for which it qualifies concerning the hiring of its personnel." Earlier in his decision, he stated, "Because AiG likely qualifies for the ministerial exception under Title VII, it can choose to hire people who adhere to certain religious beliefs while still being in compliance with state and federal law as agreed in the application and without their hiring practices being attributed to the Commonwealth."

The ruling is strange because it seems to apply to AiG and not to the Ark Encounter, the actual business that is hiring and the park at which the employees would be working. In trying to understand the ruling, it might help to know that Judge Van Tatenhove is a George W. Bush appointee and thus is someone likely to side with Christian organizations in cases such as this one. Notably, the judge waited to make his ruling until after the outgoing Democratic governor had left office and Matt Bevin, a Tea Party Republican, had become governor. In turn, Bevin fired most members of the Tourism Board, replacing them with more like-minded individuals. Granted, Bevin did nothing illegal, but his actions sure did turn out to benefit Ken Ham greatly. The new board quickly approved the $18 million tourism tax credit.

The judge all but ignored a 2004 Supreme Court ruling, *Locke v. Davey*, in which the court ruled that states actually have the legal right to disallow religious organizations from participating in tax-related programs. Had the judge looked at that ruling, he would have been forced to rule in the state's favor. Further, if the state had decided to appeal his decision, it could have easily won on those grounds.

I was asked right after the ruling if I felt that I had lost. I did for a moment. I felt rather defeated, especially in the context of our massive victory the previous year. I thought we had prevented Ham from taking advantage of the tax benefit and upheld one of the founding principles of our country. The state government had made the right decision. I didn't foresee that an activist judge would overturn our work and that a new governor who doesn't care about religious freedom would support the judge's decision. It took a lot of effort for them to skirt the Constitution and that reaffirms for me that we were right all along. Ham may have won the court case, but he and his crew lost months of time battling our efforts. While this is not the victory we hoped for, we did make a clear statement that illegal practices won't go unquestioned and that the Christian Right's religious privilege is coming to an end.

Currently, there are no legal options for us to pursue unless a potential employee decides to challenge the hiring practices in court or Kentucky taxpayers themselves try to sue the state to stop the unlawful usage of tax money. Yet, I don't feel discouraged by this outcome. I still feel inspired to keep fighting. I am especially encouraged knowing how much I learned from this process—lessons that will help me on future missions. Further, I know we won once and, in the end, we can win again.

Indeed, the battle continues. Activists in the area mobilized immediately and planned a protest for the opening day of the Ark Encounter on July 7, 2016—a protest attended by myself, David Silverman, and many other prominent names in the secular movement. The protest did not occur to say the project shouldn't exist. Rather, the protest highlighted the fact that the park is scientifically inaccurate and called attention to the taxpayer money being used to make the park possible. If the media was going to be there to see the opening of the park, we wanted to be sure they heard not just voices of opposition— but also the truth. We also wanted to change the story the media told. We succeeded in both fronts.

Even so, I know Ham is walking around with his head high thinking he beat the evil atheists, but that is a delusion that won't last. Remember his estimate that 2 million people would visit the park each year? An estimated four thousand people showed up opening day. By the afternoon, the queue for tickets at the entrance was empty. If that's the best attendance the park could muster in a week that witnessed coverage on NBC News, NPR, and countless other national media outlets, then even the Hunden Report figures may be high. The low turnout shows that people are simply not interested in the park. As attendance drops, the park will eventually close. And when it does, I'll be there to watch Ken Ham do a walk of shame back to his crumbling Creation Museum.

As the Ark Encounter experience reminds, real change comes from a marathon, not a sprint. We must keep pushing forward—collectively and individually—to bolster the wall of separation between church and state and to secure a secular future for our country and world. To do so, as I will detail in chapter 5, we should use all available tools and resources at our disposal.

Notes

1.   Billy Hallowell, "'Not a Mention of God': This Is What a 'Secular Invocation' Looks Like," *Blaze*, June 4, 2015, http://www.theblaze.com/stories/2014/06/04/not-a-mention-of-god-this-is-what-a-secular-invocation-looks-like/.

2.   Hemant Mehta, "Secular Invocation Delivered in Longwood, Florida," *Patheos*, September 13, 2015, http://www.patheos.com/blogs/friendlyatheist/2015/09/13/secular-invocation-delivered-in-longwood-florida/.

3.   Dan Arel, "Ken Ham's Ark Encounter Loses Tax Incentive," *Patheos*, December 10, 2014, http://www.patheos.com/blogs/danthropology/2014/12/ken-hams-ark-encounter-loses-tax-incentive/.

4.   Bristol Palin, "Kentucky Pulls Tax Credits from Noah's Ark Park Because It's 'Too Religious,'" *Patheos*, December 30, 2014, http://www.patheos.com/blogs/bristolpalin/2014/12/kentucky-pulls-tax-credits-from-noahs-ark-park-because-its-too-religious/.

5.   Ken Ham, "What's Happening to America's Free Exercise of Religion?" Answers in Genesis, January 19,

2015, https://answersingenesis.org/culture/america/whats-happening-to-americas-free-exercise-of-religion.

6. Answers in Genesis, "Religious Discrimination Lawsuit Filed Today by AiG/Ark Encounter against Kentucky," press release, February 5, 2015, https://answersingenesis.org/religious-freedom/religious-discrimination-lawsuit-filed/.

7. Ken Ham, "Propaganda War Against the Ark," Answers in Genesis, January 22, 2015, https://answersingenesis.org/ministry-news/ark-encounter/propaganda-war-against-the-ark/ (accessed June 24, 2016).

8. See http://www.argconsumer.com/industry.html.

9. See http://hundenpartners.com/.

10. This research was done in part by myself and Americans United and further investigated by Tracey Moody, who is following the developments of the park closely for the Friendly Atheist blog.

11. Tracey Moody, "What Ken Ham Isn't Telling You about Ark Encounter Funding," *Patheos*, November 11, 2015, http://www.patheos.com/blogs/friendlyatheist/2015/11/11/what-ken-ham-isnt-telling-you-about-ark-encounter-funding/.

5

ACTIVIST TOOLKIT

Activism is not a one-size-fits-all activity. If there is one thing I hate, it's when one type of activist puts down other activists who are not doing things "the right way," "the proper way," etc. We should all realize activists fit very different molds, have very different skill sets, and have varying amounts of time they can contribute. It is hard to criticize a parent who works full time to support a family and who spends much of their free time with their family for only being able to post status updates or attend protests once in a blue moon. Yet, activists who devote their lives to a cause often struggle to understand why others don't care as much as they do, without realizing others do care as much, if not more, but often have personal restraints on how much they *can* do. Not everyone can give up their job, or find a job fighting for the causes they care about. Even for those who make a living as activists, they too must juggle life, family, and friends with their activism.

It is up to each individual to decide for themselves their level of involvement. To this end, every activist should ask themselves two questions:

- Are you doing as much as you want for your cause?
- Are you doing as much as you can for your cause?

If you answer yes to both, you're doing great. If you answer no to one or the other, maybe it is worth considering whether you might support the cause in other ways that better match your passion, skills, and time. It is also okay to realize you just don't want to make activism a priority. Even assuming you have the time, not everyone is cut out or has the passion for such work. But if you realize you want to be doing more and can, then do it! Don't let anything or anyone hold you back. Go out and give your all. Again, this could mean you donate money, you donate time, or you do other things for the cause that are better suited to you and your personal situation. This will mean many different things to many different people.

In this chapter I highlight some of the ways that you can help promote secularism, along with some of the secular groups you can work with to accomplish even more. This should not be seen as a be-all-end-all list but rather as a resource to help facilitate your journey as a secular activist.

Petitioning

When I was involved with animal rights activism, I worked on a campaign in California called Proposition 2. The goal was to improve the lives of animals inside factory farms by removing battery cages for chickens and gestation crates for pigs. To do this, we needed to first get on the ballot, and to get an initiative on the California ballot, you need a lot of signatures.

Now, many of the signature gatherers you typically see are paid. They make money per signature gathered. This was a practice we decided not to follow. We wanted the signature-gathering campaign to be volunteer only because we knew any money we saved in that stage could be used to promote and defend the proposition later. The initiative was a success. We got the measure on the ballot and it passed.

The Christian Right has no problem using petitions and ballot initiatives. This is how the Mormon Church fought to get Proposition 8 on the California ballot,[1] which was a vote to define marriage as being between one man and one women and to overturn a California Supreme Court ruling that had legalized same-sex marriage in the state. The church spent obscene amounts of money to make sure this initiative passed. They may have used the ballot-proposition system for evil, but just imagine what we could do if we used such systems for good. Oregon residents did when they voted to approve the state's Death With Dignity Act.

Each state will have its own laws regarding petitions and propositions for voters, but if you have the time and resources, pursuing such initiatives is a great way to encourage voter involvement in ending religious privilege in many areas.

Letter/Email Writing

This is really old school, but get a group together and write letters or emails and slam local businesses or politicians, or whoever your target is, and make your voices heard. These communications do get opened, and even if the U.S. president or your congressperson or state representative doesn't personally read them, someone on staff does. Elected officials periodically receive reports about the issues their constituents are writing to them about, which in turn can have an impact on their policy decisions.

Sometimes a single letter can get the job done. Phil Ferguson, host of a secular-themed podcast called *The Phil Ferguson Show*, tells a story about how his daughter's public school was promoting a Christian breakfast in the mornings before school started. Of course, underprivileged kids would go to take advantage of the free food they desperately needed, even if they had to be preached to just to enjoy a much-needed meal. Well, Phil decided to offer the same thing, but from a secular perspective. A free meal with no preaching.

The school originally refused his offer but thanks to a

crafty letter the school finally agreed to promote the secular alternative, before later deciding to just stop promoting both.

Blogging/Writing

Blogging and any form of journalism are great ways to get a message out there. The easiest way to start is to sign up for a blogging system such as Tumblr, WordPress, Blogger, or the many other sites that are totally free and let you blog away. You can start writing on topics you care about and share them on social media and try to build a following.

Ideally, you should first write for someone who already has a readership and thus can help you reach more people quickly. This is not too difficult to do as it only takes emailing site admins and editors and telling them who you are and why you want to contribute to their site. For example, sites like Atheist Republic, which reaches millions through social media, are always looking for new talent who have something to say.

I'll tell a quick story about how I got my start to show that it can be done. You can use it as a sort of template or motivational push. Initially, I blogged for myself. I would clear maybe eighty readers a month if I was lucky. I would write and write and write, yet no one would read my work.

I was then introduced to a site called Emily Has Books, which was full of writers discussing important atheist and secular issues. I emailed Emily, shared some of my work, and told her why I wanted to write for her. My first piece for her had over a thousand readers, and I could not believe it. I wrote there for a few months and caught the attention of someone at the Richard Dawkins Foundation for Reason and Science. I wound up writing there a few times, which in turn led to my work against Ken Ham.

It all started because I sent one email to one editor and asked to make my voice heard, and things grew from there. Today I am sitting on my couch writing this, which will be my second book. Not too bad for a young guy who not too long ago was blogging for eighty readers a month, in a good month.

The point here is, blogging is a great way to make your voice heard and gain momentum. People like Ham don't want their misdoings written down and documented, and you can do just that. You can make life rather uncomfortable for people who don't want to be caught taking advantage of the system.

Slacktivism (or Online Activism)

Activism comes in many different shapes and sizes and you should not feel discouraged if you cannot get involved in large national campaigns or even smaller local ones. Not everyone wants to go speak in front of city council or get into a head to head with someone like Ken Ham, but you may still want to be active and do your part.

This is where slacktivism comes in. You know those people who never do or say anything political but suddenly change their profile picture to an equals sign to stand up for same-sex rights? Or people who don't march in antiwar protests but post about being antiwar all day long? Those are slacktivists, and they are often discredited as being lazy, but they are in fact important parts of the activist community, because they get messages out, trigger dialogue, and show solidarity.

I often think of my own mother in this case, who rarely if ever posts anything about politics on her Facebook wall, but who one day changed her profile photo to an equals sign. I debated someone on social media that same day about the usefulness of such gestures; they argued they were meaningless, but I argued such gestures play a much larger role than people give them credit for. For example, when my mom changed her profile picture that day, she was communicating to her network of friends that she supported equality. As a result, perhaps friends of hers felt a new connection to her, or perhaps those who disagreed with her but respect her took a second to reflect on their own feelings on the issue.

The very debate I had about slacktivism was a form of slacktivism. I did not change the mind of the person I was publically communicating with—they were dead set in thinking such gestures were useless—but I saw numerous "likes" coming in on my comments and realized people were following the debate as it happened. Some agreed with me, and some did not, but I knew people were reading and knew I had the potential to change minds or at the very least to make people think about what they believed.

So what can you do as a slacktivist? You can do plenty, and thankfully there are plenty of tools to help you be an effective one.

Facebook

Facebook is one of the easiest ways to make your voice heard online. You can share articles, join groups, and have discussions with people around the world about issues you care about. Don't be shy about sharing your opinion; be bold and willing to have discussions. The hardest part about any online activism is keeping your cool when you encounter the absolute worst of people. The important thing to remember is often you're not going to change the mind of the person you're debating with, especially if the debate is about religion or politics. But remember that many people can be watching and many may not have a position on the issue or are on the fence about it, so how you present yourself and the evidence for your case is important. If you flip out and tell someone off, it may come across that you don't have a strong case for your position, which makes the other side look better. You will flip out sometimes, and some people will just rub you the wrong way or not care to have an open and honest discussion, but try your best to remember why you do what you do and that minds can be changed, even if not today.

Even if you don't enter into debates, just sharing an article about keeping classrooms secular or supporting marriage equality shows others where you stand, which in turn may help them uncover where they stand on the issue or force them to evaluate their own views. Never forget that you have the power to change minds—don't be afraid to try.

Twitter

Twitter may be my favorite social media platform because it connects people from around the world with so much more ease than Facebook; you don't even have to be friends with people to interact with them. It also has a 140-character limit and forces people to have more focused thoughts, so they can't ramble on like they can on Facebook.

Twitter has great search features that let you find tweets and respond to them. I used to do a daily search for terms such as atheist, atheism, and evolution and then would address those tweets that seemed sincere but that were totally wrong. Or, on really boring days, I'd look for those that were just totally insane and have fun with them, but that's a different subject.

For tweets that say something like, "atheists have no

morals because they don't have a bible," tweet a response publicly explaining why atheists do in fact have morals and that morality does not come from a book of rules. Again, you are unlikely to change the mind of the tweeter, but you can rest assured your tweet will be seen by others. Much like on Facebook, the minds of readers can be changed.

Great tweeters are out there for inspiration too. Donovan Badrock tweets as @MrOzAtheist and does an amazing job questioning religious assumptions and correcting negative ideas about atheism. @GodFreeWorld is a professor of biology and takes a great deal of time out of his day to address those who incorrectly tweet about evolution or defend creationism. His tweets are often educational for everyone reading, not just for the creationist. He has taught me a great deal about evolution even though I studied it in school! I could go on and on and on about amazing tweeters you should follow, but they are not hard to find.

In addition, Twitter is a great resource for any atheist to connect to the online atheist community and to learn more about atheism, science, and secularism and to see what battles are being fought in all different parts of the world. With Twitter, you are opened up to the whole world. For example, you can connect with atheists living in the Middle East who can't even tell their own families they are atheists, but who speak freely on Twitter.

Twitter is one of the easiest yet most powerful tools available to every type of activist. Use it to your advantage.

Movements

For those looking to help others through writing or fundraising—or even by simply raising awareness—there is a very cool site called Movements (movements.org). The idea is to crowdsource activism, to provide a space where people, generally those actively oppressed in the Middle East, can post their story and ask someone to help them tell it. If you're a blogger looking to help and need story ideas, Movements is full of them, and you can do a great deal of good with them.

YouTube

For those of you who don't mind a little extra work but still want to sit in your favorite chair, there is YouTube. The site offers a great way to make your voice heard and address social issues and has the potential to reach large audiences. Video interview shows, social commentary, informational videos, and humor all go a long way to further the cause. For inspiration, I recommend the Bible Reloaded, which read through every single book in the Bible. Though not appropriate for all ages, the show is hilarious and one of my favorites. Creationist Cat is another clever show that rips on religion while making social commentary. It is so insanely dumb I cannot stop watching—I mean, it's a cat that is a creationist. Aron Ra and Mark Nebo put on an amazing show and podcast called Ra-Men, which has some of the best guests. Aron also tackles some of the biggest subjects in his solo videos and does a great deal to spread the fight for secularism and science education.

You don't have to start big. Record what you have to say and share it and if people like it, it will catch on.

Other

There are many other ways to make your voice heard online, such as through an Instagram account that shares memes and information, a podcast, a Vine, or a Periscope. Be creative in the ways you reach people and you will see results. Not everyone has to take down a giant to make a difference. Simply make your voice heard and tell people what you think they should know, and hopefully many will join you and get involved as well.

Even if you do nothing but talk only to your friends and family, that is a start. Many people vote and pick candidates based on information they receive from their social networks, so why not make your views known, especially if someone you know is on the wrong side of an issue.

The point is, if you're interested in being involved, there are ways to do it. You don't have to be out in the streets or devoting the better part of your day to it if you don't want to or simply can't. You can be an activist in your own time and on your own terms. Don't be discouraged by those who want to make you feel bad for not doing more. Often the ones who criticize activists the loudest are the ones who do the least amount of work.

Secular Organizations

It is usually not possible to go it alone in a fight against the government or corporate giants, and you should never have to. I did not take on Ken Ham by myself. Indeed, I would have accomplished very little if I had tried to do so. Thankfully, we don't have to take on these fights alone in the secular community. We have an outstanding number of local and national groups that are ready and willing to help. They are also eager for you to join them as a volunteer so that you can help others as well. I will highlight just a few of the many organizations that are essential in every secular activist's life.

Americans United for the Separation of Church and State

Americans United was founded in 1947 and is one of the longest standing and more important secular watchdog groups on this planet. They work tirelessly to monitor religious liberty and to respond to church-state violations and have played an instrumental role in upholding the secularity of this nation.

They have fought to keep religion and creationism out

of schools, to stop religious schools from receiving taxpayer money through school voucher programs, and to keep churches from becoming political outposts.

As already noted, they also played a leading role in the battle against Ken Ham.

American Atheists

American Atheists is one of the leading U.S.-based nonprofits that focuses on protecting the rights of atheists and normalizing atheism. In addition, they also fight to uphold religious freedom for all religions by making sure the wall between the separation of church and state stays standing. They realize that without religious freedom there is no protection for atheists, Jews, Muslims, or any other religion that is outside of the majority.

American Atheists is also not afraid to take on unpopular causes necessary for upholding secular principles, like suing the 9/11 Museum for putting up a cross, a move that saw the organization smeared on every national channel you can think of. The lawsuit may not have been the popular choice but it was an important one. They understand that Christianity cannot be set loose to make its own rules and that they must try to keep the majority in check, no matter the negative attacks they may face in response.

Freedom From Religion Foundation

Like Americans United and American Atheists, the main goal of the Freedom From Religion Foundation (FFRF) is maintaining the separation of church and state and educating the public about nontheism. They often send letters to public schools, government officials, and others who may be illegally promoting religion in the public sphere. They have an active member base of activists willing to monitor and respond to reports of church-state violations around the country.

They have also been very involved in the Ark Encounter case, working to highlight the dubious if not illegal fundraising activities of Answers in Genesis, which accepted tax-deductible donations for the Ark Encounter. FFRF sent a letter to the IRS highlighting the legal issues behind such a tactic, but sadly the IRS did nothing, as they do in almost all cases regarding religious organizations breaking the law.

Secular Student Alliance

The Secular Student Alliance (SSA) works with high school and college students to help them set up their own secular groups to not only bring like-minded people together but also to provide an active voice for secularism in schools and communities. Many of the cases picked up by Americans United, American Atheists, and the Freedom From Religion Foundation stem from SSA student groups, who may see discrimination or a church-state violation on campus or in their communities and take action.

Many other groups actively work for secular causes. They include the Richard Dawkins Foundation for Reason and Science, the Center for Inquiry, and National Center for Science Education, which do great work in education; Foundation Beyond Belief, which helps secular groups raise money for doing good around the world; the Secular Coalition for America, which focuses on promoting secular policies; and Atheist Alliance, Openly Secular, and Recovering from Religion, which help support those leaving the abusiveness of religion.

A simple Google search will yield many other secular groups, whether national organizations that are working for the betterment of the country as a whole or smaller groups that offer local support and opportunities. If you get involved in a battle with a religious group or organization and need support, these and other organizations are ready to help you.

Notes

1. Prop 8 was illegal from the get-go. Thankfully the courts agreed and overturned the ballot initiative shortly before the U.S. Supreme Court legalized same-sex marriage.

6

A CALL TO ACTION

When I wrote *Parenting Without God*, I ended it with a call to action for parents to come out publicly as atheists if it was feasible for them to do so without risking their financial stability or safety. I wanted to tell those parents in hiding that they should not be afraid to come out if they feared only personal rejection or rejection for their kids at school. I wrote:

> *If you are an atheist hiding just because life may get harder, I would like to talk to you about coming out, especially if you are a parent. Yes, for some, this may make life a little more difficult. Being out means you have to tell friends, family, coworkers, etc., that you do not believe in God, that you are not religious, and so on.*
>
> *More importantly, though, is that change comes when numbers grow. Atheism is becoming more and*

more common, and as more people feel the desire to come out and speak up, the less odd it will be for someone to know an atheist.

It's a funny thing to think that some people don't know, or, at least, think they don't know an atheist. Atheists are like aliens to some people. I believe we have a responsibility to come out. When we live in a country and a world where so many atheists cannot come out safely, those of us who can have a duty to come out and change the false image of atheism.

We cannot do this from the closet. Change will not happen if we are all hiding from the world and afraid that we may get poked at or that our kids may be called names in school.

That passage, I believe, contains the most important message in the book—the idea that we can eliminate the stigma of parenting without God simply by coming out and saying we are doing so. This, to me, was a massive call to activism. Come out and change the world was my message then, and it still is today. Strength lies in numbers.

My plea to you, my whole reason for writing this book, is not to tell you how great I am for trying to stop Ken Ham,[1] because I am not. I am an activist who hitched on to something that needed to be done, who saw it through, and who is still seeing it through. To me, writing this book is part of my activism, because

I want to share my experiences just as others did to inspire me. I want to encourage new and veteran activists to not only stay committed but to also embrace others and their activism—to stop the whole "I'm a better activist than you" mentality that engulfs almost every movement. My hope is for people to read my words and realize that anyone can do this, and then for those same people to actually step up and do it. I want those who pick up this book to be my comrades and to fight alongside me in our battle to remove religious privilege from our communities and to strengthen the wall of separation between church and state. We are making real progress on many fronts.

Yet, we, as a movement, have a lot of work ahead of us. To tackle the issues ahead, to look forward, we need you in our ranks. We need people willing to do the work and to make real change in this country—including to attain true gender and sexual equality. Many say such issues are not "secular" causes, but they truly are, because most of their root causes are religiously based. Gender inequality, specifically as relates to reproductive rights—along with discrimination against the LGTBQ community—stems in large part from religion. The Christian Right believes they have a right to enact laws that make certain classes of people second-class citizens. In addition to these causes, we also need to combat rampant systemic racism and the systematic slaughter of people of color by our law enforcement.

Our nation was founded on the principle of religious freedom, yet today's Christian Right believes religious freedom applies only to Christians. As I write this, Donald Trump, as part of his presidential campaign, has called for all Muslims to be banned from entering the country and suggested we keep a national database of Muslims inside the United States. While such statements garnered plenty of uproar, they also catapulted him to the top of the Republican presidential nomination process.

The response to such statements from the Christian Right, those crying the loudest about religious freedom, is a deafening silence. Religious freedom for Muslims is under attack and yet you hear crickets from them. Worse, you see growing evangelical support for Trump. The Christian Right does not care about religious freedom or the separation of church and state, and they most certainly do not care about secularism. In fact, many hate it. Former Arkansas Governor Mike Huckabee has called secularism antagonistic toward Christianity and has charged that atheists want to impose a secular theocracy: "That's it. It's humanistic, atheistic, even antagonistic toward Christian faith. And that's what we need to understand. Our basic, fundamental rights are being robbed from us, taken from us piece by piece."[2]

The Christian Right, while still shrinking, has the numbers to sway elections, politicians, and policy, and they truly believe their own nonsense. They believe secularists are going to come knock on their doors and take away their Bibles and ban them from practicing their religion. They tell researchers that they trust us less than they trust rapists, and hell, they even told Pew pollsters that they would vote for a Muslim before they would vote for an atheist, and they hate Muslims!

And when it comes to hatred of atheists, we even have work to do within our own ranks, thanks to the regressive left and journalists such as Max Blumenthal, Glenn Greenwald, and Nathan Lean, all of whom blame atheists, or specifically, "new atheists," for violence against and hatred toward Muslims. Atheists such as myself, Sam Harris, Richard Dawkins, Michael Sherlock, and others are told we are oppressing Muslims by speaking out against Islam. They claim we are wrong to say that Islamism is a consequence of religious belief. They have no issue with us saying that a Christian who shoots up a Planned Parenthood is a Christian terrorist, but if someone yells "Allahu Akbar" before running into a building and killing people, don't you dare blame religion.

These are the same people who blamed the *Charlie Hebdo* staff for their own deaths on January 7, 2015, when two Islamist gunmen walked into their office and opened fire. These regressive leftists believed that because the satirical magazine drew what seemed like insulting magazine covers about Muslims, they had brought the terror down on themselves. They also accused them of racism—without ever taking a single second to understand the French political climate or what the covers drawn by the *Charlie Hebdo* staff truly represented. It was much easier for these faux-leftists to blame the victim rather than to admit there is a problem of violence within Islam.

This ideological rhetoric and white-savior complex not only places the blame for right-wing extremist attacks against Muslims on atheists, but it also makes Muslims less safe in their own countries because the regressive left won't allow criticism of the very foundation of the oppression many of them are living under. The number one victim of groups like ISIS are Muslims. Saudi Arabia's barbaric practices are wielded against other Muslims. We know religion plays a role in this, yet when we state this transparently clear fact we are called racists and bigots. We are told that only America and its allies are to blame for every social and cultural ill and that religion has nothing to do with any discriminatory or violent act done in the name of Islam. We have our work cut out for us here.

Looking ahead, we have many goals. We want to remove the idea that a business can hold a religious belief, as we learned after Hobby Lobby. We want to make sure state and local officials do not ignore the Supreme Court ruling that legalized same-sex marriage. Women's rights continue to be under attack as states continue to find new ways to restrict clinics such as Planned Parenthood, all in an attempt to stop them from having the ability to perform abortions. As we have seen time and again, the Christian Right doesn't care about the lifesaving and important medical services such clinics perform outside of abortions; they are more than willing to remove all female health services because of their religious ideology. They call themselves pro-life, but they are anything but.

We must confront the pro-life movement, or more correctly the anti-abortion movement, on a regular basis. They regularly use rhetoric such as "murderer" and "baby killer" to describe doctors and clinic employees and offer a religious justification for religious fanatics to walk into these clinics and open fire. We saw this in 2015 in Colorado Springs, Colorado, when a man named Robert L. Deer shot and killed three people at a Planned Parenthood clinic, including a police officer responding to the call. Deer was quoted as saying, "No more body parts," when police finally arrested him. His comment was in reference to a widely publicized video released by an anti-abortion group that claimed Planned Parenthood was selling baby body parts for profit. The accusation proved to be amazingly untrue; the video had been highly doctored. Despite this, Republican politicians such as Carly Fiorina and the anti-abortion movement continue to make these and similar claims, with inevitably deadly results.

We must also fight for transgender rights, work to make trans people feel more accepted, and do all we can to curb the suicides happening in the community, as these young men and women fight to feel accepted by our society. I have conversations weekly with religious people who refuse to accept trans people and continue to claim that being trans is a mental illness or that someone cannot be a gender different from their biological sex at birth. They refuse to accept gender as fluid or as a social construct.

We must battle this ignorance with facts. We must keep having these horrible conversations and telling people the truth about what it means to be transgender and what gender is. We must also tell them it doesn't matter how they feel about the issue, because trans people exist, and they are killing themselves in absurdly high numbers, in part because of the negative attitude many religious people have toward them. We, as a species, as a society, can do better than this. We owe it to everyone to do better than this.

We must keep working to stop creationists from disrupting our classrooms by trying to force their nonsense into the minds of children or by lobbying to remove evolution from the classroom. We are going to defend proper scientific education and call out the bunk that is creationism or intelligent design and raise our children to be scientifically literate. We will not let these cretins bully our school boards or harass our teachers.

We won't let government officials pander to the Christian Right, allow loopholes to sneak religion into our schools, or find sneaky ways to fund private schools with taxpayer money.

We must certainly continue to fight against those like Ken Ham who get taxpayers to pay for their sectarian projects. If they try to pretend their projects are nondiscriminatory or hide behind cries of "religious freedom," we are going to be there to pull the mask off and show the bigotry they are disguising. We are not going to let taxpayer dollars build giant, useless, landlocked boats or other structures to worship their chosen god. We are not going to let taxpayer money go to someone like Ken Ham, who continually asks for cash yet reportedly takes home nearly $200,000 a year in income and pays the rest of his family $300,000 a year to spread ignorance around the world.[3]

And we are going to win every single one of these fights because we are without a doubt on the side of right. Our drive and passion for creating a just and equal world make us unstoppable. Our ability to adapt and change with the times gives us an advantage over those clinging to an archaic belief system that is more antiquated than alchemy. We understand society evolves and we are willing to flow with this evolution. Gender identities, sexual norms, and even language change with the times. We do not rely on religious texts or a supposed dictator from above telling us what we should do or think.

Rather, we look at issues through the lens of fresh evidence and a healthy dose of skepticism, along with plenty of empathy and compassion. We also recognize that questions of gender and sexual orientation are specific to each individual and do not have bearing on the lives of anyone else, thus accepting gender fluidness and sexual orientation should be simple.

Our future looks fantastic because we are already winning. Religious affiliation is dropping, the religious stronghold on our government is weakening, and we are poised to return this government to the bastion of secularism it was always intended to be. We lost a lot of ground during the days of the Moral Majority and in years after, but we have never given up. Thanks to groups like Americans United and American Atheists we never stopped fighting, and thanks to activists through the generations and people just like you and me, we are going to keep pushing forward until the disease that is religion is removed from our government once and for all.

This won't be easy, and it will be a long struggle, but we know it will be worth it. We also know it will be necessary. I have no doubt we will all, together, accomplish great things. Some of you will become activists like the ones I have described in this book, and some of you may even get directly involved in politics. Indeed, I hope this book leaves you motivated and feeling that you can do great things. I never imagined I would be in a position to discuss a victory like the one I had, but because I had a passion to keep going, and the help of such great people, it happened. I want it to happen for everyone else, because only together can we win this fight. My victory was only a small piece of a much bigger fight. It will take many more victories to dramatically change the course of this country, but each victory knocks a block from the foundation the Christian Right is built upon. Before long, we will chip away enough that the whole thing will come crumbling down.

Now I want you to go out there and become the activist you want to be and the activist I know you can be.

This fight is ours.

Notes

1. But please, don't hesitate to let me know!

2. David Edwards, "Mike Huckabee: 'God's Blessing' Will Make Me President to Stop the Atheist 'Secular Theocracy,'" *Raw Story*, January 22, 2015, http://www.rawstory.com/2015/01/mike-huckabee-gods-blessing-will-make-me-president-to-stop-the-atheist-secular-theocracy/.

3. Dan Arel, "Answers in Genesis Pays Ken Ham and Family $500,000 a Year," *Patheos*, December 14, 2015, http://www.patheos.com/blogs/danthropology/2015/12/answers-in-genesis-pays-ken-ham-and-family-nearly-500000-a-year/.

ACKNOWLEDGMENTS

This book would not have been possible without the patience shown and freedom granted by my amazing wife, Danielle, who spent many nights watching Netflix without me while I was glued to my computer writing this and other countless articles. She does an amazing job raising our two kids, London and Luella. The spouse of a writer takes on a much larger burden than most people will ever realize.

Along with my entire family and my friends, who offer endless encouragement and support, I also want to thank Kurt Volkan, who brought my first book back to life when the original publisher went under and who believed in this project enough to work with me again.

I also thank everyone at Americans United, especially Rob Boston, who never ignored a single email I sent him; David Silverman of American Atheists for the Foreword and for his tireless work and guidance; and Danielle Muscato, an activist in every sense of the word and a force to be reckoned with who I am glad to have on our side.

I want to extend my deepest gratitude to Casper Rigsby, who helped edit this book and offered his insights to make it better throughout the process. Rigsby's work with Atheist Republic is helping create the next generation of activists.

I absolutely must thank Amanda Knief and recommend her book *The Citizen Lobbyist*. I took great inspiration from her writing and modeled my own book to some extent after hers; I loved her how-to approach for inspiring lobbyists and I hope to do the same for inspiring activists.

And lastly, I must thank David Fitzgerald. When I walked off the stage at Apostacon 2015 after delivering my speech on the Ark Encounter project, he walked up to me and said, "This needs to be a book." Well, here it is, David.

FURTHER READING

Some of you will want to know more about activism, different forms of it, different applications, and different ways to discuss these issues with people out in the public. I have compiled a small list of highly recommended books that will be beneficial to your journey.

The Citizen Lobbyist by Amanda Knief (Pitchstone Publishing, 2013)

A Manual for Creating Atheists by Peter Boghossian (Pitchstone Publishing, 2013)

Letters to a Young Contrarian by Christopher Hitchens (Basic Books, 2005)

Faith Versus Fact by Jerry Coyne (Viking, 2015)

Fighting God by David Silverman (Thomas Dune Books, 2015)

God & Government by Rev. Barry W. Lynn (Prometheus Books, 2015)

Attack of the Theocrats! by Sean Faircloth (Pitchstone Publishing, 2012)

Necessary Trouble by Sarah Jaffee (Nation Books, 2016)

Socialism . . . Seriously by Danny Katch (Haymarket Books, 2015) Note: I don't recommend this book in an attempt to make you a socialist; rather, I recommend this book because it helps shed light on how activism has changed over the years and offers a vision for enacting change in this nation through activism.

ABOUT THE AUTHOR

Dan Arel is an award-winning journalist and bestselling author of *Parenting Without God*. He writes full time for his Patheos blog Danthropology, covering religious and political news. He has a column in *American Atheist* magazine and contributes to *CounterPunch*, *Huffington Post*, and *Time*, and previously served as an editor and columnist for the Richard Dawkins Foundation for Reason and Science. He lives in San Diego, California.